Centenarians

Centenarians

One Hundred 100-Year-Olds
Who Made a Difference

Dale Richard Perelman

SEVEN LOCKS PRESS

Santa Ana, California
Minneapolis, Minnesota
Washington D.C.

Seven Locks Press
P.O. Box 25689
Santa Ana, CA 92799
(800) 354-5348

Individual Sales. This book is available through most bookstores or can be ordered directly from Seven Locks Press at the address above.

Quantity Sales. Special discounts are available on quantity purchases by corporations, associations, and others. For details, contact the "Special Sales Department" at the Seven Locks Press address above.

Printed in the United States of America

Library of Congress Cataloging-in-Publication Data
Perelman, Dale Richard
    Centenarians: one hundred 100-year-olds who made a difference / by Dale Richard Perelman
        p.   cm.
    ISBN 0-929765-70-2
        1. Centenarians–United States Biography. 2. Centenarians Biography.
3. United States Biography.   I. Title

CT215.P47   1999   99-41761
305.2'092'273–dc21   CIP
[B]

Cover & Interior Design: Sparrow Advertising & Design
Editorial Services: PeopleSpeak

The author and publisher assume neither liability nor responsibility to any person or entity with respect to any direct or indirect loss or damage caused, or alleged to be caused, by the information contained herein, or for errors, omissions, inaccuracies, or any other inconsistency within these pages, or for unintentional slights against people or organizations.

Dedication

To my wife, Michele

CONTENTS

Part I—Twenty-Three Special Centenarians 1
George Abbott—*Broadway and Film Director,*
Producer and Actor. 3
Irving Berlin—*Noted Composer* 8
Edward L. Bernays—*Father of Public Relations* 14
James Hubert "Eubie" Blake—*Musician and Composer* . . 21
George Burns—*Raconteur, Actor and Writer* 26
Frederick Carder—*Founder of Steuben Glass.* 29
Amasa Gleason Clark—*American Pioneer* 32
Sarah Delany and Bessie Delany—*African American*
Trailblazers 37
Marjory Stoneman Douglas—*Author and*
Environmentalist 42
Eleanor Lansing Dulles—*Author, Educator and United*
States Diplomat 49
Hamilton Fish—*United States Congressman* 57
Madame Chiang Kai-Shek—*Author and Diplomat.* 62
Rose Elizabeth Fitzgerald Kennedy—*America's Best*
Known Mother. 71
Alfred Mossman Landon—*Governor and Presidential*
Candidate 80
Lee Meriwether—*Author and Free Thinker* 84
Sir Moses Montefiore—*Philanthropist.* 91
Joseph Tilden Montgomery—*A Voice of the Old West* . . . 98
Grandma Moses—*Primitive Folk Artist* 102
Scott Nearing—*Author, Educator and Gadfly* 106
Chief William Red Fox—*A Bridge between the Sioux*
Nation and America's Past 111
George Seldes—*Journalist and Writer* 115
Beatrice Wood—*Mama of Dadaism.* 121
Adolph Zukor—*Visionary Hollywood Producer* 128

Part II—100 Centenarians Who Made a Difference 135

   Dr. Charles Greeley Abbot
   George Abbott
   Amelia Agostino del Rio
   Dr. Katherine Bain
   Evelyn Fortune Bartlett
   Preston R. Bassett
   Irving Berlin
   Edward Bernays
   Aaron Birnbaum
   Eubie Blake
   Rose Blumkin
   Dr. Harvie Branscomb
   Eleanor McMillen Brown
   William Slater Brown
   George Burns
   Irving Caesar
   Jeanne Calment
   Frederick Carder
   Philip Lord Carret
   Amasa Gleason Clark
   R. K. Colcord
   Dr. William D. Coolidge
   Miriam Marlin Cosel
   Hulda Crooks
   Geoffrey Dearmer
   Bessie Delany
   Marjory Stoneman Douglas
   Eleanor Lansing Dulles
   Dr. Abigail Adams Eliot
   Elizabeth Eyre de Lanux
   Gwen Ffrangcon-Davies
   Hamilton Fish
   Reverend James H. Flye
   Dorothy Frooks
   Dr. Roma Gans
   Edward King Gaylord

Delia Goetz
Esther Schiff Goldfrank
Milton Goodman
Dr. Harold Foote Gosnell
Lord Edgar Granville
Dr. Ernest Stacey Griffith
Rose Rosenbaum Hamburger
Charles W. Hargens
Dr. Charles Hartshorne
John N. Heiskell
Dr. Paul Chesley Hodges
Chester Cornelius Hoff
Ralph Horween
Jacob H. Horwitz
Ma Hsiang-Pai
Admiral Richard Harrison Jackson
Albin Johnson
Ernst Junger
Mai-ling Soong Kai-shek (Madame Chiang)
Lazare Kaplan
Rose Fitzgerald Kennedy
Alma Kitchell
Edward E. Kleinschmidt
Alf Landon
Esther Lape
Adolph Lowe
Louis W. Mahle
Marie Louise Levesque Chasse Meilleur
Lee Meriwether
Victor Mills
Lady Naomi Margaret Haldane Mitchison
Sir Moses Haim Montefiore
Joseph Tilden Montgomery
Wenceslao Moreno
Walter L. Morgan
True Delbert Morse
Christian Mortensen

Anna Mary Robertson "Grandma" Moses
Dr. Scott Nearing
Dr. Dorothy Bird Nyswander
Mumeo Oku
Marie Provaznik
Chief William Red Fox
Harold Eugene Roach
Olga Rudge
Frederick J. Schlink
George Seldes
Lord Emanuel Shinwell
Rebecca Beldner Shulman
Major General Ralph Smith
J. Roy Snyder
Sir Thomas Octave Murdoch Sopwith
Harry Stanley
Dorothy Stickney
Leon Stukelj
Charles F. Taylor
Dr. Thomas Wyatt Turner
General James A. Van Fleet
Harry E. Wedeck
Joseph Weil
Irvin Ferdinand Westheimer
Beatrice Wood
Bishop Andrew Yu Yue Tsu
Adolph Zukor

INTRODUCTION

I have promises to keep, and miles to go before I sleep.
—Robert Frost

The age of 100, attained by so few, always has held a mystical significance. Sixteenth-century Spanish explorer Juan Ponce de León searched the Florida Everglades for the mythical island of Bimini and the Fountain of Youth in hopes of discovering the elixir of eternal life.

Although the song says, "It ain't necessarily so," chapter 5, verse 27 of Genesis in the Bible assures us that Methuselah lived to be 969 years old. Such extreme longevity fascinated our ancestors and continues to transfix our imagination. Who among us has not marveled at some senior citizen who excelled as a painter, actor, philosopher, businessperson or just a golfer still capable of shooting his age? How unique it becomes when that person has attained the age of 100.

A Dr. Li, who was supposedly born in China in 1677 and died at the grand old age of 256 in 1933, received a certificate from the Chinese government attesting to his 200th birthday. Although claims like Dr. Li's undoubtably are exaggerated, centenarians have existed throughout the ages.

For some reason, inhabitants from certain remote corners of the world have experienced unusual longevity. Numerous centenarians live in the Andean village of Vilcabamba in Ecuador, the Hunza area of Pakistani-controlled Kashmir, Abkhazian in Soviet Georgia, and Azerbaijan along the Iranian border. Baptismal records from the Catholic church in Vilcabamba confirmed 9 living centenarians out of a population of 819 in 1971. A corresponding 1970 census in Azerbaijan showed 63 centenarians for every 100,000 people. As a comparison, only 3 out of every 100,000 people reached the age of 100 in the United States during the same period.

What caused this longevity? Could a healthy lifestyle be the answer? Miguel Carpio of Vilcabamba drank and smoked until well past his 100th birthday. Centenarian Khfaf Lasuria of Georgia smoked a pipe and enjoyed a daily vodka. American 100-year-old Irving Berlin smoked until late in his life, and George Burns rarely could be found without his cigar.

Most centenarians lived abstemiously by modern standards—everything in moderation. Diet appeared especially critical to longevity. Dr. Alexander Leaf in his research of areas where people lived the longest discovered that most ate sparingly. In a 1973 article in *National Geographic,* he found the long-lifed male ate approximately 2,400 calories per day and the corresponding female only 1,700. The meals contained low fat and cholesterol and high quantities of fruits and vegetables. Centenarian economist Scott Nearing gave up alcohol, meat and sweets at a very young age. As expected, the over-100 population generally was thin. Tall men such as George Abbott and Moses Montefiore tended to live longer than short ones such as Adolph Zukor. As expected, female centenarians far outnumber males.

The majority of the senior citizens Dr. Leaf investigated worked as farmers, exercising every day—primarily through physical labor. The 1990 United States census reported that Iowa, a farm state, proportionally led the country in hundred-year-olds.

Few professional athletes have reached the age of 100, possibly due to the high level of strain on their bodies. Centenarian Ralph Horween, a successful businessman and patent lawyer, played professional football for the Chicago Cardinals from 1921 to 1923 under the name Ralph McMahon. Outfielder Paul Otis and pitchers Chester Hoff and Bob Wright each played a few games of major league baseball. Congressman Hamilton Fish had been an All-American football player at Harvard in 1908–1910, but these athlete-centenarians proved the exception.

Dr. Leaf predictably uncovered a strong correlation between family genetics and long life. Most hundred-year-olds had brothers, sisters or parents who also lived to a great age. A further link between women with several children and longevity might exist. In the United States, centenarian Rose Kennedy had 9 children and Grandma Moses 10.

With modern medical treatments, an increased population base and improved diet, the trend toward longer life continues. In 1999, an estimated 70,000 centenarians lived in the United States. Today's obituaries frequently include centenarians, and I suspect ages exceeding 100 will become far more common.

Still, centenarians occur infrequently, and the following 100 thumbnail biographies of the famous and near famous should inspire us to manage our diet and stressful lifestyles so that we too can achieve the age of 100 and beyond.

*****

The author wishes to give special thanks to Richard DiGia and Susan Dexter for their line drawings.

Part I

Part I includes the stories of 23 centenarians, most of whom have achieved national or symbolic importance. They represent a wide range of people—from artists and entertainers to activists and teachers—all pioneers in their own way. Each one has been the subject of one or more books outlining his or her life.

George Abbott (1887–1995)
Broadway and Film Director, Producer and Actor

A cacophony of faultfinding and nagging haunted writer, producer, director and actor George Francis Abbott's early family years. His father, a tall, handsome, jovial two-term mayor of Salamanca, New York, and his school teacher mother clashed, constantly disappointing one another. The father proved a poor businessman and a heavy drinker. The mother lacked the warmth and sexuality the father desired.

Young George cried out for love and affection. A problem child, he reacted to his parents' lack of sensitivity to his needs with retaliatory bedwetting. Complicating his unhappiness, a severe case of granulated eyelids inflamed his retinal tissues and weakened his vision.

After the bankruptcy of his father's wholesale tailoring business in Salamanca, the family moved to Cheyenne, Wyoming, where Mr. Abbott received an appointment as a government land agent.

To help the family finances, George arose at five in the morning to deliver newspapers. Later he worked for Western Union and often carried telegrams to the red-light district, where patrons frequently sent him to the local saloon for a bucket of beer. If someone wanted 50 cents of beer, he'd order 40 cents' worth and pocket the dime.

Eventually suspended from school for unruly behavior, George landed at the Kearney Military Academy in Nebraska to cure his rebellious attitude. Living by the bugle, reveille spelled the beginning of his day, taps the end. George rebelled at the regimentation. Arriving as a private, he left at the same rank after almost two years of promotions and demotions.

When George's father lost his government appointment, he took work as a flour salesman in the east. His heavy drinking had made him increasingly unreliable, placing added financial strain on the Abbott household.

The family returned to New York, and George, although mouthy and not particularly well liked, became captain of the Hamburg High School football team. An excellent and aggressive player, he once broke a tooth on an opposing player's head. He also developed an interest in high school theater.

When George's father again lost his job as a salesman due to drinking, his mother returned to teaching to buoy the family finances. George worked summers at Lackawana Steel as an assistant electrician for 17 cents an hour over a 12-hour day, a decent wage at that time. The difficult and dangerous conditions tempered Abbott's attitude toward life and steeled his sinews. During his long days, the youth vowed never to repeat his father's weakness for alcohol.

George created another problem for himself—a pregnant girlfriend who elected to undergo an abortion rather than push for marriage. The teenage boy suffered what he called "the pangs of hell" for the pain he caused the girl and vowed to curb his impetuous nature.

In 1908, George Abbott entered the University of Rochester on an athletic scholarship. Now six feet, one and one-half inches and 170 pounds of muscle, he played tackle on the varsity football team and continued his interest in drama.

While in college, he began to experiment with creative writing. The drama club performed his play *Perfectly Harmless*. Following graduation, he attended Harvard for one year, where he wrote *The Head of the Family* for the Harvard Dramatic Club. He also won a $100 prize for his play *The Man in the Manhole*.

The call of the theater had captured George Abbott, and he departed Boston for the lure of New York City. Sharing a $3-per-week room at the 23rd Street YMCA, he met with rejection after rejection. Living on the money he made doing odd jobs and a few dollars from his mother, Abbott faced limited progress.

Eventually, Abbott's persistence paid dividends. He received a small part in a play at the princely sum of $45 per week. On the home front, he received more good news. After years of alcohol addiction and failure, George's father quit drinking and became an Erie County supervisor.

With his career moving forward, George married Ednah Levis, a Phi Beta Kappa and a school teacher, whom he had known for seven years. While George toured small theaters and played one-night stands, his wife managed her brother's law firm. All the while, George continued to write.

Within a few months, Abbott received a role in noted Broadway producer David Belasco's play *Daddies,* a major step toward his economic autonomy. He also created the lyrics for a song called "Adelai."

Eventually Abbott's career blossomed. While acting in *Dulcy,* he cowrote *The Fall Guy* in 1925. His contemporaries named him as one of the 10 best performers of the year for his part in *Zander the Great.* The show *Hell-Bent Fer Heaven,* in which he acted in 1924, received a Pulitzer Prize. Since Ednah recently had given birth to a daughter, Judith, the timing of his success was ideal.

During the next two years, he worked on nine plays as a director or writer in addition to acting in others.

Broadway, a musical he wrote and directed, provided Abbott's first "monster hit." After several more wins, he went to Hollywood in 1928 to direct a short subject called *The Bishop's Candlestick,* starring Walter Huston, the first of his 11 movies.

Abbott believed *Manslaughter,* starring Claudette Colbert and Frederic March, was the best and most believable picture he directed. While life seemed too good to be true, fortune provided a jolt. During the time he cowrote the screen story *All Quiet on the Western Front* along with Maxwell Anderson, his beloved wife, Ednah, died from cancer.

After a suitable mourning period, Abbott inched into his former social circle and began to date. Although puritanical by nature, neither drinking nor smoking, George frequently accompanied the mysterious and provocative Neysa McMein, an artist and bohemian who lived in what was then considered a scandalous "open marriage." He even sailed with her to Egypt in the winter of 1933.

Twentieth Century, a play he directed and coproduced with Ben Hecht and Charles MacArthur, generated another hit, but three failures followed in quick succession. How quickly fate can humble the mighty.

The law of compensation—out of bad times, good must surely follow—produced the fabulously successful *On Your Toes* in 1936, which featured Rodgers and Hart's "Slaughter on Tenth Avenue" and starred Ray Bolger. Abbott both cowrote and directed the production.

Next, *Room Service* with Eddie Albert exploded onto the New York scene. Abbott frequently had several shows on Broadway during any season.

Abbott's newly found fame also brought a variety of people from the past seeking a portion of his material success. Notoriously stingy, he took special pleasure in fending off their requests. The '30s also brought Abbott an appendectomy, his only brush with illness or injury since his football days.

Never a true romantic, Abbott thought little of it when he introduced Lucille Ball to Desi Arnaz on the set of his comedy *Two Many Girls.* After the two became an item, Abbott joked about being the matchmaker, although he had little to do with the natural attraction that developed during the show's rehearsals.

To overcome the pangs of middle-aged bachelorhood, Abbott wedded Mary Sinclair, a young former actress. The marriage alternated between sunshine and rain. Mary regretted leaving the theater for wedded life and envied her husband's success. In 1952, the two divorced after five stormy years. The renowned attorney Louis Nizer provided Mary with the financial settlement she sought.

However, Abbott's wealth multiplied with '50s Tony Award blockbusters such as *The Pajama Game* and *Damn Yankees.* After more than a decade behind the scenes, the writer-director returned to the stage as an actor in *Skin of Our Teeth* with Mary Martin and Helen Hayes. In 1959, *Fiorello* brought him the coveted Pulitzer Prize, the Drama Critics Circle Award and two Tony

Awards. *A Funny Thing Happened on the Way to the Forum* premiered after Abbott reached the advanced age of 75.

Over the years, George Abbott's Broadway shows provided a chain of future Hollywood stars such as Richard Widmark, José Ferrer, Carol Burnett and Van Johnson. A man of dramatic flair, technical skill and physical vitality, he wrote, directed or acted in more than 100 shows throughout his long career. The master of the snappy line was an arch-apostle of pace and timing in his plays. Famous as a "play doctor," he exhibited the ability to pull a rabbit from a hat and turn it into mink or sable. No one brought more excitement to Broadway than that creative genius known to his coworkers as "Mr. Abbott."

In 1982, Abbott received the Kennedy Center Lifetime Achievement Award. The following year he married Joy Valderrama, a former nightclub dancer 40 years his junior. The couple frequently played golf for relaxation.

During his 99th year, Abbott sent his secretary two plays he had written between rounds of golf. In 1989, the 102-year-old dynamo codirected one of the two plays, *Frankie*. His wife reported that he was dictating revisions to the second act of *Pajama Game* for a planned revival two weeks before his death.

Stiffly formal, Abbott generally dressed in a business suit and tie. He rarely spoke more than necessary. Once when a "method" actor asked, "What is the motivation for that line?" Mr. Abbott tartly replied, "Your job."[1]

Abbott believed the key to his longevity lay in an abstemious lifestyle rather than good genes, since he far outlived any other members of his family. "I do not think burning the candle at both ends casts a lovely light," he explained.[2]

George Abbott died on January 31, 1995, at the age of 107 after a long, vigorous and creative existence in which he added greatly to the luster of both the Broadway stage and the Hollywood motion picture industry.

Irving Berlin (1888–1989)
Noted Composer

Irving Berlin was born Israel Baline in Temun, Russia, on May 11, 1888, the eighth child of a poor cantor. One of his earliest memories of his native land involved Cossacks savaging his village. Flames bellowed from the rooftop of his home while he cowered in a nearby field beneath a blanket. Galloping through the streets on horseback, brandishing sabers, maiming and murdering unarmed Jews, the fearsome Cossacks torched homes for the sheer joy of it. Somehow, the Balines escaped the carnage, waiting for the marauders to sate themselves on blood and thoughtless mischief.

Israel's father, Moses Baline, recognized that Russia no longer remained a safe haven for his family, and he opted to risk his future in the New World. Although the long trip across the Atlantic remained a blur to four-year-old Israel, he would wear a deep scar on his forehead, an ugly souvenir from a knife that accidentally fell on him from a shipboard bunk.

In New York, Mr. Baline struggled with three jobs to provide food for his family. The misery of tenement life on Cherry Street of the Lower East Side, or Jewtown as it was called, and the rigors of physical work proved too much for him. He died of bronchitis before Israel's ninth birthday.

To help out with the family finances, Israel hawked newspapers after school. Once, a crane knocked him off a pier into the East

River while he was engrossed in reading a copy of the *Evening Journal*. Luckily a bystander dove into the water to save him.

Shortly after his Bar Mitzvah, "Izzy" dropped out of school and "went on the bum" to seek a career in music. He took to the Bowery streets as a guide for a barroom balladeer known as "Blind Sol," eking out a living on 25 cents a day. Within a few years the boy's soprano voice and aggressiveness took him up the ladder from saloon-hall singer to song plugger and budding lyricist.

While waiting on tables and singing at the Pelham Cafe for a Russian known as "Nigger Mike," 19-year-old Israel cowrote the lyrics for his first published song, "Marie from Sunny Italy." Although Israel and his cowriter each received only 37 cents for their efforts, the name I. Berlin, a name he selected randomly, appeared on the title page of sheet music for the first time.

Shortly thereafter, Irving Berlin lost his job at the Pelham Cafe. He fell asleep at the bar while on duty, and someone stole $25 from the till. When the owner returned, he fired Irving on the spot.

Berlin next found employment at Jim Kelly's, where Berlin wrote the words for the musical spoof "Sadie Salome, Go Home," a success that swayed the Tin Pan Alley firm of Waterson and Snyder to offer him a contract for $25 per week as a lyricist. During his first year, Berlin wrote the words for dozens of songs.

At a barber shop, Berlin asked vaudeville actor George Whiting to join him that evening for a show. Whiting answered, "Sure, my wife's gone to the country." The reply struck a chord with Berlin and provided the inspiration for his hit song "My Wife's Gone to the Country," words by I. Berlin and G. Whiting, music by T. Snyder.

In 1911, Berlin joined the Friar's Club. As a new member, he volunteered to write a ragtime song for the Friar's Frolic. Berlin adapted the spicy rhythms of the South to create "Alexander's Ragtime Band." Within a short period, the song revolutionized music, and Berlin became the "King of Ragtime."

Berlin, a street-smart promoter, combined a shrewd business mind with the genius of musical originality. His high-pitched staccato voice with its New York flattened *a*'s and mishmashed *r*'s, interspersed with a touch of sarcasm and periodic profanity, spiced up his personality. His dark eyes and broad smile balanced this rough exterior to make him likeable.

In 1912, the 23-year-old songwriter married Dorothy Goetz, the raven-haired sister of producer Ray Goetz. Following an idyllic honeymoon in Cuba, the couple moved to an apartment over-looking the Hudson River. Tragically, Dorothy had developed typhoid fever in Cuba and died within a month.

Disconsolate, Berlin thought he could never write again, but his brother-in-law encouraged him to translate his grief into music. The hauntingly beautiful "When I Lost You" in Dorothy's honor sold 1 million copies.

Busying himself in his work, Berlin commenced a prolific out-pouring of music. In 1914, he wrote the lyrics and music for the ragtime show *Watch Your Step,* starring Irene and Vernon Castle. In 1915, "I Love a Piano" headed Berlin's list of hits.

Even as Berlin's fame grew to star status and his wealth multi-plied, he continued to remember his mother. One day, after picking her up in a taxi at her modest Cherry Street flat, Berlin took her to an attractive house in the Bronx. When his mother, Leah, pointed out that suppertime was approaching and she should return home, Irving told her this was her new home.

With the advent of World War I, Berlin enlisted in the army. At five feet, six inches and weighing less than 125 pounds, the musi-cian struggled through the physical rigors of boot camp with the other recruits. When General J. Franklin Bell asked Sergeant Berlin to produce a show that would raise $35,000 for a soldier's center, he accepted the assignment without hesitation.

Berlin applied all his nervous energy to the production of *Yip Yap Yank,* which featured the smash song "Oh, How I Hate to Get Up in the Morning." The show raised $80,000, far exceeding the original goal of $35,000.

At the end of the war, Berlin and his friend Sam Harris opened the Music Box Theater on 45th Street off Broadway. Although the theater cost more than $1 million to build, it deservedly earned the nickname "The House of Hits."

In 1925, Irving met Ellin Mackay, the beautiful daughter of Clarence H. Mackay, president of Postal Telegraph and Cable

Corporation, and heiress to a $30 million fortune. Irving quickly grew to love Ellin's animated eyes, sensitive face and sharp sense of humor. She represented the ultimate symbol of status for this once-poor immigrant—blond hair, blue eyes and a society pedigree. However, Clarence Mackay did everything possible to stop his socially prominent daughter from marrying a Jew. When Mackay disinherited Ellin, Berlin merely whispered to her, "My poor darling, now I'll have to give you a couple million of my own."

When the couple gave birth to a daughter, the grandfather ignored the event. Not even the death of their son caused Clarence Mackay to relent. Only the loss of his fortune during the depression and Berlin's financial assistance created a truce between Ellin and her father.

Berlin also suffered losses during the depression, but the songs continued to pour from his fertile mind. "How Deep Is the Ocean," "Let's Have Another Cup of Coffee," "Easter Parade" and "Heat Wave" represented but a small selection. *Top Hat,* starring Fred Astaire, featured the song "Cheek to Cheek," which delivered almost $250,000 in residuals, a sum equivalent to millions of dollars in today's economy. The mid-thirties included *Follow the Fleet, Carefree* and *Second Fiddle.*

Although Irving Berlin played the piano poorly and had difficulty reading music, he could write hits. To overcome his inability to play in any key other than F sharp, he used a specially designed composing piano he liked to call his "Buick."

With the clouds of war on the horizon, singer Kate Smith asked Irving Berlin to compose a patriotic anthem. He responded with the blockbuster "God Bless America," whose royalties he donated to the Boy Scouts, Girl Scouts and Camp Fire Girls, a wonderful and generous gift.

During World War II, Berlin wrote "Any Bonds Today." Too old for active duty, the veteran warrior returned to Camp Upton, the birthplace of *Yip Yap Yank* during World War I, to produce *This Is the Army,* which would earn more than $10 million for the Army Relief Fund. For his efforts during the war years, Irving Berlin received the Medal of Merit from General George Marshall.

Holiday Inn, starring Bing Crosby and Fred Astaire and featuring the immortal "White Christmas," exploded onto the postwar musical era. *Annie Get Your Gun* in 1946 and *Call Me Madame* in 1950 kept Berlin on top of the heap. This chain-smoking dynamo with the reedy voice and the slight swagger in his step projected an aura of creative invincibility.

However, Berlin's output quickly ebbed in the '50s. Reluctantly, he put his piano in storage to concentrate on the business end of music.

Suffering from depression and shingles, Berlin became reclusive, writing only an occasional song and painting in his free time. He watched his diet and rationed his activities to preserve his strength. After almost a decade of minimal activity, he attempted a comeback with *Mr. President,* but the play lacked the energy of his earlier works.

With his composing years behind him, he spent his days protecting copyrights and looking after his publishing company.

As age took its toll on his body, Berlin retreated into his own insecurities. Late-night phone calls complaining of real and imagined ills irritated his friends. Irving Berlin, once an inventive genius with a benevolent streak, degenerated into a crotchety old man. While his eyesight deteriorated, his mind remained somewhat intact.

When an acquaintance complimented him on his appearance one morning, saying he looked like he had slept well the previous night, Berlin, a notorious insomniac, countered, "Yea, but I dreamed that I didn't."

Berlin could be magnanimous, but he also could be petty. When his nephew Irving Berlin Kahn asked for financial help for his mother's medical bills, the songwriter blurted, "She's my sister, but she's your mother. When you use up your money taking care of her and you run out, then I'll help."

As Kahn started to leave the room, Berlin issued a parting volley. "By the way, don't call yourself Irving Berlin Kahn. Use an initial. Please don't use my name."

On May 11, 1988, Carnegie Hall honored Irving Berlin with a 100th-birthday televised tribute culminating in a chorus of "God

Bless America." The aged songwriter neither watched nor commented on the program.

Less than three months later, Berlin's wife, Ellin, died at the age of 85. His expansive love for his wife had been one of the finest aspects of the man.

Following Ellin's death, the composer's health weakened rapidly. He had little to keep him going. He died on September 22, 1989, four months after his 101st birthday, far outliving any of his relatives. President George Bush described him as a "legendary man whose words and music helped define the history of our nation."[3]

Morton Gould, the president of ASCAP (American Society of Composers, Authors and Publishers), summed up the composer's greatness: "Irving Berlin's music will last forever. Not for just an hour, not for just a day, not for just a year, but always."[4]

Edward L. Bernays (1891–1995)
Father of Public Relations

Born in Vienna, Austria, in 1891, Edward L. Bernays, the father of public relations, descended from an illustrious family. His great-grandfather had been chief rabbi of Hamburg and a relative of the poet Heinrich Heine. Edward's mother, Anna, was the sister of the noted Austrian psychoanalyst Sigmund Freud.

When the Bernays family immigrated to the United States in 1892, Edward spent his first birthday aboard ship. He enjoyed a happy but controlled childhood in New York City, believing himself to be his mother's favorite as the only boy in the brood of five children.

Edward's early diet certainly played a small role in his longevity. He later recalled with relish his mother's gargantuan dinners featuring hearty soup, thick roasts and heavy desserts accompanied by wine. The rich cooking must not have hurt the family's health. Most of the members of the Bernays family lived well past 80.

Edward's authoritarian father, a grain broker, selected the Cornell University College of Agriculture for his son. Bernays discovered he had little in common with his farmer classmates, but he enjoyed editing the "Cornell Countryman," the school of agriculture's monthly newsletter. Four years of college passed swiftly, in which he honed his writing and thinking skills.

Following graduation, Bernays wrote for the *National Nurseryman* and worked with a grain dealer for short periods of time. While helping to edit a medical journal, he became interested in a play about syphilis called *Damaged Goods*. He both co-produced and handled the publicity for the play, whose theme was to educate the public on the dangers of the dreaded disease.

Damaged Goods opened new horizons for 23-year-old Edward Bernays, who accepted a position as a theater publicity agent for the firm of Klaw and Erlanger. He learned to add excitement to his stories to ensure proper press coverage, but he also maintained an "objective" distance from his clients.

Although Edward's choice of vocation disappointed his father, Bernays persevered in the field of public relations, which is both an art and a science—a science in that it utilizes the laws of psychology, an art in that a spark of inspiration frequently plays a key role.

In 1915, a Cornell classmate asked Edward to handle the publicity for several Metropolitan Opera stars including Enrico Caruso and Anna Case, the beautiful soprano who later married Clarence Mackay, president of Postal Telegraph and Cable Corporation and the unwilling father-in-law of future centenarian Irving Berlin. To publicize the ballet *Scheherazade,* Bernays photographed one of his stars in full costume with a live snake wrapped around her neck, a provocative portrait that caused a sensation throughout the world of opera. Bernays claimed that the intrigue and tumultuous relationships between the operatic titans "taught me more about life than I have learned from politics, books, romance, marriage and fatherhood in the years since."[5]

With the onset of World War I, Bernays joined the Foreign Press Bureau after flunking the physical for active military duty due to weak eyesight and flat feet. His assignment included the arrangement of a meeting between Tomas Masaryk of Czechoslovakia and Ignacy Paderewski of Poland to protest Austrian-Prussian world domination.

Following the armistice, the bureau selected Bernays to attend the Paris Peace Conference, a training school in the study of people and public opinion for the young publicist. He quickly learned the importance of research in public affairs. As a case in point,

Lloyd George, the prime minister of England, had difficulty dealing with Woodrow Wilson, the American president. When George commissioned a psychological sketch of Wilson, he discovered "When resolutely opposed, he yields,"[6] a fact George used to great advantage during the conference. The study of psychological profiling would prove to be an invaluable tool in Bernays's analysis of public thought.

While in Paris, Edward purchased a box of Cuban cigars, which a friend on leave in Vienna delivered to his Uncle Sigmund Freud as a gift. Dr. Freud returned the favor by sending a copy of his book *The General Introductory Lectures to Psychoanalysis,* written in German and inscribed "in grateful appreciation of a nephew's thought of his uncle."[7] Sigmund Freud's lectures added further to Bernays's understanding of human behavior patterns.

Upon returning to America, Bernays conducted a governmental public relations campaign for the re-employment of veterans. Colonel Arthur Woods of the War Department praised his efforts. "Your work has been instrumental in getting the facts before the public in such a way as to help enormously."[8] Bernays also hired a translator and publisher for Freud's lectures with the dual goals of popularizing psychoanalysis in the states and returning the proceeds of the book to his uncle.

Setting up a small public relations shop on 48th Street in New York, Bernays hired his close friend Doris Fleischman, a topnotch Barnard graduate and assistant editor of the *New York Tribune.* Working in close proximity to this attractive and spirited woman, Edward soon found that he and Doris had become soul mates and sweethearts. Their early clients included the Committee for the League of Nations, Venida hairnets and the NAACP (National Association for the Advancement of Colored People) convention in Atlanta, where Bernays feared both for his own safety and that of the participants due to the antiblack sentiment permeating the South during the '20s.

In 1922, Edward Bernays married Doris in the chapel at the municipal building in Manhattan. His wife retained the name Fleischman for business purposes, becoming the first married woman to receive a passport under her maiden name.

The year 1923 brought forth the publication of *Crystallizing Public Opinion,* in which Bernays defined the public relations profession. To expand the business community's understanding of the field, his firm issued the newsletter "Contact" to more than 15,000 potential clients, and Bernays lectured at New York University's (NYU's) School of Journalism to promote public relations as a profession. His book *Propaganda* in 1928 further delineated his philosophy.

In addition to their busy work life, Bernays and his wife frequently entertained large groups at their home, including Chaim Weizmann, president of the World Zionist Organization; Alexander Kerensky, onetime leader of Russia; and attorney Clarence Darrow.

Bernays occupied himself in a variety of interesting public relations projects. He developed a "Welcome Stranger" campaign to overcome tourist fears of violence in New York City and designed a backdrop of bold Georgia O'Keeffe paintings to dramatize Cheney Brothers silks. Since one relationship frequently led to another, a Cheney Brothers fashion show led to a longtime association with the noted jeweler Cartier. The partnership began at the magnificent Fifth Avenue building with Monsieur Cartier's admonition "You must not forget, my dear Mr. Bernays, that in this establishment discretion rules."[9]

In 1924, Bernays served as counsel for public relations for the Cartier-inspired French Exposition in New York. He received the Diplome de Haut Concours decoration from the French government for his efforts. The following year, Bernays traveled to Paris as a commissioner for the United States Department of Commerce to report upon the International Exposition of Modern Decorative and Industrial Arts.

Rhinelander Waldo, a former police commissioner of New York who had worked with Bernays on the "Welcome Stranger" campaign, retained the public relations expert to combat Alice Roosevelt Longworth's widely quoted quip that President Calvin Coolidge "was weaned on a pickle." Bernays set up a White House brunch that included noted entertainers such as Ed Wynn and Al Jolson. As Bernays introduced each guest to the president, the president shook hands perfunctorily and said "Good morning" with an expressionless look. Apparently, President Coolidge was humorless, and all the public relations efforts Bernays could muster would not change that fact.

Bernays hired the architect of Rockefeller Center to design soap sculptures for Proctor and Gamble's Ivory soap. To promote the appetite-reducing quality of tobacco, he arranged for photographs of slender female models smoking beneath the headline "Reach for a Lucky instead of a sweet." He led the campaign for a United States government stamp to commemorate the 50th anniversary of Edison's electric lightbulb for General Electric.

When the stock market crashed, Bernays became a member of President Hoover's Emergency Committee for Employment. Unfortunately, the committee only recommended rather than initiated action. Unemployment increased from 4 million to 8 million between 1930 and 1931.

To enhance the image of pearls, the public relations expert imported a sheik from Bahrain to dramatize the allure of genuine oriental pearls. Visiting Cartier, the Cultured Pearl Association and President Roosevelt at the White House, the sheik generated a great deal of excitement but did little to stem the growing popularity of cultured Japanese pearls.

Following the end of prohibition, Bernays promoted "beer as the beverage of moderation" for the beer distillers association. He penned the pamphlet "Speak Up for Democracy" for the Veterans of Foreign Wars. *Time* called it "one of the longest ads we ever saw." For Dixie Cups, he advanced the sanitary benefits of paper cups.

Edward Bernays first met Eleanor Roosevelt in 1944, when he proposed a letter campaign to re-elect the president. He also suggested having *McCalls Magazine* publish her autobiography in installments.

At the behest of Clare Boothe Luce, a beauty with dancing eyes, a keen mind and a feel for the times, Bernays led the opposition against the Daughters of the American Revolution's refusal to permit singer Marian Anderson, a black woman, to perform in Constitution Hall in Washington, D.C. After the successful completion of an antibigotry editorial campaign, Miss Anderson sang "The Star Spangled Banner" to the applause of thousands.

Bernays helped Golda Meir draft a speech to the United Nations General Assembly opposing Arab aggression. The address stressed the importance of an independent Israel to the Middle East, relying on logic rather than mere sentimentality. Golda Meir received a booming ovation.

Douglas Gilbert of the *New York World-Telegram*, eulogizing the importance of Edward Bernays to his profession, wrote an article headlined "Farmer fertilizes America's mass mind" in which he said, "He has been called the Baron of Ballyhoo, a Barnum with a psychologist's degree."[10]

In 1955, Bernays wrote "The Engineering of Consent" in the *American Academy of Political and Social Science Annals*. He edited and contributed to a book of the same name in 1947. Bernays served as the editor of the *Public Relations Quarterly* and as a guest editor for the *Saturday Review of Literature* issue on propaganda and censorship. He frequently lectured on public relations at a variety of prestigious institutions including Yale, Cornell and Penn State.

A believer in the value of education, Bernays wrote *Your Career in Public Relations* in 1947 to encourage young people to enter the field. In 1949, New York University named Bernays an adjunct professor of public relations. The following year, the University of Hawaii selected him as a visiting professor.

As he grew older, Bernays involved himself in a variety of civic and charitable functions. In 1956, Mayor Robert Wagner appointed him chairman of the Senior Citizens Committee of New York. He also served as counsel on public relations to the commissioner of the Department of Commerce of New York, acting on behalf of dignitaries such as Emperor Haile Selassie of Ethiopia, Queen Elizabeth of England and Premier Nikita Khrushchev of Russia.

As proud as he was of his accomplishments in the field of public relations, Bernays was an ecstatic father. He gloated over the attainments of his two daughters, Doris, the older, a cum laude graduate of Radcliffe, and Anne, a Barnard graduate.

Throughout his career, Bernays accumulated a variety of honors. For his 70th birthday, Mayor Wagner presented him with the Medallion of Honor to recognize his civic contributions to the city of New York.

Bernays refused to succumb to old age. He authored *Biography of an Idea* in 1965. At the age of 85, he wrote a column called "Viewpoint" for the *Public Relations Quarterly*.

Preaching the gospel of public relations as a profession, Bernays proposed a college-level educational program emphasizing writing, communication and the social sciences. Effective public relations involved the science of analyzing trends, predicting consequences, counseling organizations and implementing programs of action serving both the organization and the public's interest. He lobbied for state and federal public relations licensing.

Edward Bernays fittingly spent his 90th birthday at the Public Relations Society of America's meeting in Chicago, promoting himself and the profession of public relations to all who would listen. When asked the secret of his longevity, he stooped over and whispered in the ear of a female public relations friend, "I always kissed the girls."[11]

Active through the last year of his life, Edward L. Bernays, the dean of public relations, died in Cambridge, Massachusetts, on March 9, 1995, at the age of 103. During his lifetime, Mr. Bernays had raised his field from its infancy to a mature profession in the business world.

James Hubert "Eubie" Blake (1883–1983)
Musician and Composer

James Hubert "Eubie" Blake was born on February 7, 1883, in Baltimore, Maryland, the son of a poorly paid stevedore and a mother forced to take in laundry. His father had been born as a slave in Virginia. "My parents were proud, decent God-fearing black people, and they instilled a pride in me that has lasted for a long, active lifetime," Eubie reminisced.[12] He had loved music as long as he could remember. The rhythm of ragtime, born from the black man's suffering, surged through his veins.

Eubie's mother took her four-year-old son to the grocery store late one Saturday to take advantage of the weekend final close-outs. When Eubie heard organ music from a nearby store, he felt drawn like Ulysses to the beguiling sound of the sirens. After a few minutes of instruction, he played a simple tune.

"Ma'am, that boy is a natural," the salesman began his pitch. Although her husband had been out of work for days, Mrs. Blake, beaming at her talented baby boy, took a precious dollar bill from her purse and handed it to the salesman as a down payment. The company delivered the organ on Monday afternoon.

Soon, Eubie began taking "pie-ano" lessons from a woman who lived up the street. He developed into a quick learner, and Lewellen Wilson, a local orchestra leader and a neighbor, taught him how to write music.

Eubie's friends nicknamed him "Mouse" because of his tiny stature. Since he couldn't fight well, the guys looked after him. In fact, Joe Gans, who would win the lightweight boxing championship of the world in 1902, happened to be one of his closest buddies.

By the time he reached the age of 13, Eubie fancied himself one of the top piano players in the city, but an older teenage rival "wiped him out" and took his girlfriend during a ragtime playoff. This only encouraged him to work harder so he could play "walking bass," or what today is called "boogie woogie."

Eubie's first real job involved sneaking out his bedroom window at night to play piano at Aggie Shelton's Bawdy House. He rented a pair of long pants for 25 cents from a boy at the local pool hall to get the job. Every morning he would sneak back into the house before his father awoke for work at five in the morning.

When a woman informed his parents, his mother asked, "How do you know that it is Eubie playin' at that place?"

"Don't nobody play ragtime like Eubie," the woman answered.[13] When Eubie's father discovered his son had saved $90, more than he could make in two months on the docks, he allowed the boy to help with the family finances.

Eubie's mother continually fretted for her son's soul. After Mrs. Blake watched her son perform in Atlantic City, Eubie asked how she liked the show. "Son, it's lovely. There's only one thing wrong. It would be so much nicer if you was doing this for Jesus."[14]

"Yes, Mamma," Eubie answered with a twinkle in his eye, "but Jesus don't pay nothing."[15]

During the next few years Eubie drifted from show to show. He earned 50 cents per day plus meals at Doc Frisbee's Snappy Medicine Show. He danced in a production of *In Old Kentucky* prior to landing work at the Academy of Music in New York City.

Eubie's first wife, Avis Lee, two years his senior, had lived near him in Baltimore. When he first saw Avis, Eubie told his best friend, Hoppy, he would marry Avis some day. After Hoppy advised Avis of Eubie's plans, the girl smacked Eubie with his music book. Undaunted, Eubie told Avis he intended to marry her anyway, and he did a decade later.

In 1907, Eubie played at the Goldfield Hotel, the "swellest place in Baltimore," owned by his friend Joe Gans and a man named Eddie Meyers.[16] Eubie proposed to Avis after finishing a show at the hotel.

Madison Reed became Eubie Blake's first partner, and the two often sang "Alexander's Ragtime Band," the hit song of another future centenarian, Irving Berlin. Berlin frequently visited their show in Atlantic City. He would shout from the audience, "Hey, Eubie, play my tune."

Eubie's friends consisted of musicians, toughs, athletes and bookies. Travel, crazy hours, alcohol and tobacco made life intriguing. Like most blacks during the decades after the turn of the century, Eubie suffered the effects of discrimination. Following a race riot in Baltimore, he moved to New York. Although Eubie performed at the Cotton Club in Harlem, he was refused admission as a guest.

In 1915, Eubie teamed up with Noble Sissle, the beginning of a lifetime collaboration. The two struck gold with the song "It's All Your Fault," performed by the incomparable Sophie Tucker.

Sissle, nicknamed the "absent-minded professor" by Avis, continually forgot details. A World War I injury and subsequent surgery necessitated by an automobile accident hampered his thought processes but never his musical skills. Noble and Eubie produced hit after hit. The Schubert Brothers and Flo Ziegfeld would pay the pair a tremendous $400 to $500 for a show.

Borrowing costumes from Frank Fay and Eddie Leonard, Eubie and Noble produced their first Broadway show, *Shuffle Along,* on a shoestring. The two composers wrote the music to fit the costumes. "Bandana Days" corresponded with the plantation-style clothing from Leonard's show *Roly-Boly Eyes.* The audiences thrilled to "I'm Just Wild about Harry." Against overwhelming odds, *Shuffle Along* became a smashing success. Singer Al Jolson loved the music, frequently bringing as many as 20 people with him at $2.50 per head, a hefty price when the average worker earned 15 cents per hour.

Sissle, the better businessman, wisely insisted upon copyrighting the show. One night, when the lead attended a funeral, Eubie selected an unknown Paul Robeson to sing the part. Although the bright lights blinded Robeson, who tripped on the stage, he became an overnight sensation.

After the success of *Shuffle Along*, Eubie and Noble celebrated by taking their wives to London, where a producer with a flop hired them to write a couple of songs. They responded with "Tahiti" and "Let's Get Married Right Away" to save the show.

After nine months of full houses and encores, Eubie became homesick. Although Noble begged him to stay, Eubie refused. "I'm going home. I don't see any colored people hardly."[17]

Unwilling to break up the winning team, Noble accompanied Eubie back to the states. They joined a vaudeville tour with the Keith circuit at $600 per week. Although other performers received more money, they appeared with white stars like Georgie Jessel and Ted Lewis and liked the work. The two also wrote the musical *Elsie* during their spare time.

Life seemed to be flowing smoothly for Eubie until his beloved Avis Lee died from tuberculosis, as had her father and brother. He immersed himself in his music to hide his sorrows.

In 1930, Eubie worked on a show with a man named Andy Razaf. Years later, while Sissle and Blake starred in a musical review in Los Angeles, Eubie visited Razaf, then seriously ill. His good deed paid a rich dividend. Razaf introduced him to a beautiful, light-skinned woman named Marian, who stole his heart in an instant.

While on the road, Eubie wrote Marian almost every day, using a dictionary to check his spelling, never one of his strong points. He proposed through the mail, convincing Marian to join him on tour prior to moving to New York as his wife.

When the two traveled to Memphis, where Eubie was performing, a policeman harassed Blake for dating a white woman. In Norfolk, the couple applied for a marriage license on December 27, 1946. "Is that a white woman?" the clerk snarled. "Do you think I'm dumb enough to bring a white woman down here in Virginia to marry?" Eubie countered.[18]

Later, Eubie joined a USO tour through the South, taking Marian with him. However, the presence of the light-skinned

Marian created so much difficulty on the segregated trains that the show manager forced Mrs. Blake to return to New York.

In the '50s, Eubie Blake began to slow down his performance schedule. In the '60s, he enrolled at New York University to study the Schillinger composition system for three years after retiring from the road. From time to time, he would perform, and his 1969 appearance at the Newport Jazz Festival led to a retrospective of his music, *The Eighty-Six Years of Eubie Blake*. In 1972, he founded his own record company, Eubie Blake Music, releasing several recordings of his own and of other ragtime musicians.

Serenely happy and uncomplicated, Eubie Blake and Marian lived happily in their aging Stuyvesant Avenue brownstone in Brooklyn. Surrounded by hundreds of mementos and photographs, Eubie shut out the cacophony of the New York streets with the simplicity of his accustomed surroundings.

After years of long nights, Eubie usually slept late into the morning. Upon awakening, he often ate a light breakfast and sneaked a cigarette or two. He had given up liquor for almost 25 years. He first tried to substitute tea for alcohol, but when that didn't work, he switched to root beer, and it succeeded.

While well into his 90s, Eubie would take the number 26 bus to Schrafts to stock up on candy and donuts, an indulgence he relished on a weekly basis.

With more than 600 compositions, Eubie experienced a degree of fame. Jazz aficionados appreciated his classical ragtime style and chromatic chord progressions. "Charleston Rag," "Troublesome Ivories" and "Chevy Chase" became standards in the repertoires of the great pianists of the '20s and '30s. However, the Broadway show *Eubie* brought Eubie Blake real public notice. In June 1978, when Eubie performed on the White House lawn, he stole the show. The old pro had lost none of his magic.

Although his legs weakened with age, Eubie remained strong and alert, playing and performing until his death on February 12, 1983, a few days after his 100th birthday. The sweet memory of Eubie Blake's music and his zest for living remain a monument to his long years.

George Burns (1896–1996)
Raconteur, Actor and Writer

When 16-year-old Louis Phillip Birnbaum married 14-year-old Dorothy Bluth, the two were barely more than children. Two years and two children later, the couple emigrated to New York from eastern Europe to seek a better life. Working in a sweatshop as a pants presser on the lower east side of New York, Birnbaum struggled to support his growing family of 12 children: Morris, Annie, Isadore, Esther, Sarah, Sadie, Mamie, Goldie, Nathan, Sammy, Theresa and Willy.

Life proved difficult, but Dorothy Birnbaum worked to provide a traditional Jewish home for her family. When Nathan rigged a looped wire to steal seltzer bottles from a neighbor's porch, his mother made "her son the thief" return the bottles and apologize. Although Nathan's father, a religious man with a long gray beard and kindly brown eyes, died at age 47, his mother continued to teach him right from wrong.

Nathan, or Natty, whom we came to know as George Burns, tried to joke his way through poverty. He claimed that Luigi the organ grinder provided him with his first taste of show business. At age seven, George joined the Peewee Quartet, singing on street corners for throw money. At the Cooper Department Store amateur contest, the quartet won an Ingersoll watch for their rendition of "When Irish Eyes Are Smiling."

As a child, George would pick up pieces of coal from the street to take home. Friends, seeing his knickers bulging with coal, would call him the "Burns Kid," a reference to the local coal company. The nickname stuck, and George kept the Burns name for the stage.

George quit school in fourth grade to become a singer, dancer and trick roller skater in vaudeville. He even did an act with a seal. His career stalled until age 27, when he talked a pretty little Irish singer with a natural talent for comedy named Gracie Allen into teaming up with him. On January 7, 1926, George and Gracie also became man and wife between appearances in Cleveland, Ohio. "It was a short wedding and a short honeymoon, but a long and wonderful marriage," George reminisced.[19]

George's pal Jack Benny recommended the team of Burns and Allen for a Warner Brothers short. Soon, Paramount signed them to four shorts at $3,500 each. In addition, the couple earned $750 per week in vaudeville. At last, the couple had struck the financial big time.

Their first full feature, *The Big Broadcast,* starring Bing Crosby, Kate Smith and Cab Calloway, came in 1932. Numerous movies followed in quick succession: *International House* with W. C. Fields, *College Humor, Six of a Kind, Many Happy Returns, Big Broadcast of 1937, A Damsel in Distress* and *College Holiday,* to name a few. George and Gracie's comedic genius reached international fame with *The Burns and Allen Show,* which lasted on radio for 19 years.

In 1950, George and scatterbrained wife Gracie began an eight-year run on CBS television. George, following the format of the noted play *Our Town,* acted as the narrator, describing the zany antics of his wife, while feeding her straight lines. George always had the last laugh—he got to bank the paycheck. The television program always ended with George's "Say good night, Gracie," and her predictable response of "Good night, Gracie."

When Gracie retired in 1958, the show ended and George worked alone. In 1964, Gracie died from a massive heart attack. She had been George's love, his best friend, his partner and companion for the better part of four decades.

"I only had one joke for 40 years, and then she died," George wrote, burying his grief in humor.[20]

At age 79, the cigar-chomping, gravel-voiced comedian overcame heart surgery to begin a second career, playing opposite Walter Matthau in *The Sunshine Boys,* which won him an Academy Award as best supporting actor. The movie *Oh, God!* by Larry Gelbart starring John Denver in 1977 became extremely successful. George would walk into a restaurant and waiters would ask questions like "Would God like two olives in his martini?" *Just You and Me, Kid* with Brooke Shields and *Going in Style* with Art Carney and Lee Strasberg followed in rapid succession.

In 1988, George played a grandfather whose body is switched with his grandson's in *18 Again.* During that same year, he received a John F. Kennedy Center for the Performing Arts lifetime achievement award. In addition, he wrote *Gracie: A Love Story,* which became a best seller. The following year he wrote *All My Best Friends,* a collection of remembrances about his show business buddies, "a pretty good book for a guy who only read two of them."[21] Burns's recording of "Gracie" also won a Grammy.

Good health and a wonderful outlook on life made George Burns one of the world's most popular centenarians. When a reporter asked him if his doctor knew he still smoked, Burns joked, "No, he's dead."

George drank moderately, watched his weight and smoked only an occasional cigar. Since he far outlived his parents and siblings, luck rather than good genes added to his years. He promised to play the London Palladium at age 100, refusing to die before that magic age since he was "booked." Unfortunately, he fell in a bathtub a few months prior to his birthday and was forced to cancel the performance.

George Burns died quietly in his Beverly Hills home on March 9, 1996, shortly after his 100th birthday. His wonderful sense of humor, as it is showcased through his movies, television career and books, continues to be an eternal inspiration to his millions of fans.

Frederick Carder (1863–1963)
Founder of Steuben Glass

Artist, chemist and glassware engineer Frederick Carder was born of middle-class parents in Staffordshire, England, in 1863. A serious youth, Frederick turned down the opportunity to attend Oxford or Cambridge at the age of 14 to shovel coal at his father's pottery works. At night he studied drawing, casting, design and metallurgy at the Stourbridge School of Art and the Dudley Mechanics Institute. He spent what free time he could garner sketching famous glassware and carving marble and glass.

While still in his teens, Carder left his father's plant to become a designer for the firm of Stevens and Williams, art glass specialists. He spent almost two decades honing his skills in creating colored glasses and also served as the company's international salesman.

Throughout his years at Stevens and Williams, Carder retained his connections with the Stourbridge School of Art. In 1891, he formed the Wordsley School to train talented glassmakers in drawing and advanced production techniques.

In 1902, the Stourbridge School sent Frederick Carder to Germany and Austria on a fact-finding mission. The following year, he went to the United States to assess the country's glass-making skills.

While in Corning, New York, Carder met T. G. Hawkes, who provided him with the financial backing to set up a factory for the production of undecorated handblown glass "blanks" to feed his engraving company. Carder hired Swedish workers from a competitor and founded Steuben Glass, the first glass company in the United States to install a coal-fire furnace.

With experimentation and practice, Carder and his company created a variety of colored and opaque art glasses including Verre de Soie, which featured a rainbow play of color caused by a tin chloride spray, and Aurene, a unique and beautiful golden irides-cent glass, whose name derived from *aurus,* meaning gold, and *shene,* the Old English word for sheen. Heavily influenced by Roman and Egyptian works and the Victorian and Art Nouveau periods, Carder developed Millefiori (one thousand flowers) glass around 1915.

With the advent of World War I, resource shortages forced Steuben Glass to close its doors temporarily, and Corning Glass acquired the financially troubled Carder holdings.

Frederick Carder became the art director for the newly expanded firm. He gained a reputation as a problem tackler and creative innovator. During his free time he often golfed with Dr. Eugene Sullivan, the president of Corning Glass.

Over the next decade, Steuben Glass created a variety of interest-ing glasses: alabaster, amethyst, Cluthra bubble glass, moonlight and plum jade glass. However, Carder believed Intarsia, a colored glass sandwiched between two thin layers of crystal, represented his greatest achievement. Today, the world's largest collection of Steuben glasses rests in the Rockwell Gallery, owned by Robert Rockwell, a friend of Carder and a former Corning executive.

As early as 1900, Carder served as a delegate to the Congress of Chemistry at the Paris Exhibition. In 1925, he joined the Hoover Commission, dedicated to the development of the New Art Exhibit in Paris. The Royal Society of Arts in London elected him to a fellowship, and he served on the advisory committee of New York's Metropolitan Museum. He founded the Corning Rotary Club and became its first president. A past president of the Corning City Club, one of the founders of the Corning Country Club and past president of the Corning Board of Education, on which he served for 25 years, Carder actively pursued a variety of civic and artistic activities. Carder held an honorary doctorate from Alfred University. The Architectural League of New York awarded him its Friedsam Gold Medal, and the American Ceramic Society presented him with the Binns Medal.

By the late '20s, business at Steuben had begun a serious decline. The depression in the '30s caused sales to plummet. Carder ignored the public's taste for colorless glass, and his stock of unsold iridescent product accumulated.

A memo to the president of Corning from another executive stated the problem: "Certain deficiencies are apparent in plant organization, cost planning, morale, working conditions, sales assistance and general co-operation. It is clear that a change must be effected within a comparatively short time if continued and increasing losses are to be avoided."[22]

In February 1932, a bitterly disappointed Carder was forced to resign many of his day-to-day responsibilities at the insistence of the company president. However, the peppery-tongued executive frequently visited the plant to make his feelings known to all who would listen. He formally retired in 1959 at the age of 96.

Escaping most of the infirmities of old age, Frederick Carder retained the ability to identify his works by year of manufacture until his final days. He played a fine game of golf, shooting a 90 on his 90th birthday, a very respectable feat. After a full and vibrant life, this grand old man of glassware died on December 10, 1963, a few months past his 100th birthday. The beauty and creativity of Frederick Carder's Steuben designs will last forever.

Amasa Gleason Clark (1825–1927)
American Pioneer

Born on September 3, 1825, in Schoharie County, New York, Amasa Gleason Clark lost his mother to illness before his fifth birthday, a major turning point in his life. His father, a farmer who once had served on a reception committee to honor the Marquis de Lafayette, the French hero of the Revolutionary War, remarried after a suitable mourning period. However, Amasa developed a strong dislike for his stepmother, an austere woman who sought to control the boy's rebellious nature.

On May 13, 1846, the United States Congress declared a state of war with Mexico, associated with the annexation of Texas. Relations between the countries had deteriorated until President James Polk felt forced to order troops into the disputed territory between the Nueces and Rio Grande rivers. The 20-year-old Amasa Clark, who welcomed any reason to get away from his stepmother, enlisted in the army. After feeding the oxen their morning hay, he departed the farm on foot for his military indoctrination at Governor's Island without any goodbyes. He asked a neighbor to tell his father and younger sister where he was going.

Training on the base proved rigorous. For a $12.50 bounty and the promise of 160 acres of farmland, Private Clark slept on a stone floor with only a blanket and an overcoat for protection from the elements. Following a breakfast of light bread, fat bacon and thick, syrupy coffee, he drilled for hours in 12 inches of snow.

Within the month, Clark found himself a member of the Third Infantry in Point Isabel, Texas, under the command of General Winfield Scott, prepared to invade Mexico.

In March 1847, Amasa marched south to take part in the siege of Veracruz against General Santa Anna's army. Having positioned his artillery batteries, General Scott sent a messenger under a flag of truce requesting all women and children to evacuate the city prior to bombardment. For eight days the Mexicans heroically withstood the onslaught of more than 6,000 shells and a loss of 1,000 lives. The American forces triumphed.

U.S. troops routed the Mexicans at Cerro Gordo. Although General Santa Anna managed to escape, word spread through Amasa's platoon that the Mexican leader had left behind his wooden leg and a chest of more than 100,000 silver dollars during his hasty retreat.

While the Americans continued their pursuit deeper into Mexico, they encountered a virulent plague at Jalapa. Amasa and dozens of his comrades grew ill, and the doctors could find no cure. A physician who examined Amasa Clark thought he surely would die. Fortunately, the young soldier's natural bodily defenses allowed him to recover, and he rejoined his regiment at Puebla.

Throughout the war, the Mexicans valiantly opposed the intruders from the north. While admiring the bravery on both sides, Amasa Clark witnessed the ugliness of the battlefield. He watched close friends die. At Mexico City, a German soldier who fought at Amasa's side lost a finger. Scores of men of the Third Infantry suffered from cholera after eating raw green corn. The hanging of a trio of deserters proved especially painful, causing Amasa to have nightmares for weeks. In addition to the bullets, the violence, the disease, the exhaustion from the long marches and a lack of sleep, the unbearable heat savaged Amasa's body and soul.

At the gates of Mexico City, Clark scaled the walls of the castle at the forefront of his troops while a cohort raised "Old Glory." The next day General Scott marched into the city's central square while a band of U.S. soldiers played "Yankee Doodle." The war had ended.

Although Amasa Clark abstained from liquor his entire life, he drank a glass of brandy to celebrate the American victory.

Suddenly, the buildings swayed, and several Mexicans fell to their knees in prayer. Amasa recalled, "I was sure I was drunk, but the saloonkeeper yelled out 'earthquake.'"[23]

In June 1848, Amasa marched to the city of San Antonio, where he again became ill. After recovering, he returned to his company in time to face a flood and another cholera epidemic. Dozens of victims died and had to be buried without benefit of a coffin to prevent the spread of the contagion. Private Clark's commanding officer, General Worth, was among the dead.

The army released Amasa a few months after the final battle. On the back of his discharge paper, his sergeant wrote, "Private Amasa Clark distinguished himself for bravery and good conduct at the bombardment of Veracruz, the battles of Contreras, Churubusco, Molino del Rey, Chapultepec and street fighting in the city of Mexico."[24] His commander, Major Henry, affixed his signature to the paper.

To support himself, Amasa labored at a variety of menial jobs: shoveling rocks at the Old Alamo, hauling freight or peddling goods in exchange for chickens, milk and eggs. Food rarely proved to be a problem since game was abundant. Deer, turkey and other birds could be found everywhere. Once he found a bear cub and raised it to "a good size." Unfortunately, a young boy killed his pet, who actually was quite docile.

Life in the West could be difficult. Amasa recalled a time he received a canteen of buttermilk that tasted funny. When he poured out the contents, he discovered a dead rat.

Killings and robbings were frequent occurrences in Texas at that time. Bands of marauding Indians occasionally attacked settlers on the outskirts of town.

Amasa Clark began hauling shingles for a living. While camping out for the night during an ox-train delivery to San Antonio, a band of robbers ambushed the sleeping haulers. They murdered one of Amasa's companions and seriously injured another, who later died from his wounds. Amasa lay battered and unconscious for hours. When he awoke, badly stunned, he managed to load his injured friend on the wagon and get him to medical help. The doctor expected both men to die, but Amasa survived, although it took him years to recover.

Amasa Clark married Eliza Jane Wright, a friend of the doctor who had saved his life, on July 10, 1859. After 24 years of wedded happiness, Eliza died in 1883 at the age of 42, having borne her husband 10 children, 9 of whom lived past infancy.

One of the first settlers in Bandera, Texas, Clark purchased a 1,600-acre farm in 1869 in exchange for a six-shooter and a yoke of oxen. He learned to grow fruit, primarily pears, reaching a peak output of 3,000 bushels during one season.

Amasa enjoyed the peace and solitude of farm life. Since population was sparse and "neighbors" frequently had to travel many miles to visit one another, guests often stayed for several days.

In 1885, Amasa fell in love again and remarried. His wife, Lucy Wedgeworth, gave him 8 children and 40 years of happiness.

As the years passed, numerous organizations recognized Amasa Clark's longevity. The Pioneer Freighter's Association named him an honorary vice president for life. The Veterans of Foreign Wars invited him to their annual convention in San Antonio, where General John Pershing personally greeted him.

Amasa Clark remained healthy until the last year of his life. His hearty appetite had not diminished with age. At the age of 99, he performed farmwork chores, including the digging up of tree stumps in his orchards. His mind remained sharp. He could still describe the quality and productivity of the output of various fruit trees.

Clark's younger sister almost joined her brother as a centenarian. She reached the age of 98 but died before her brother's 100th birthday.

As Amasa's important birthday neared, he took an active interest in the planning of an appropriate celebration. His wife, 16 living children, 86 grandchildren and 70 great-grandchildren gathered to watch him cut a cake containing 100 candles.

The Pioneer Freighters presented him with a gold medal. "I don't know why I lived so long, but God has his purpose," Clark explained to the family and friends who came to pay their respects.[25]

Amasa Clark died from acute indigestion on January 28, 1927, at the age of 102. His friends campaigned successfully to erect a monument in his honor at Fort Sam Houston Cemetery, consisting of a rough boulder with the coat of arms of his beloved Third

Infantry, in which he served during the Mexican War, and a tablet from the Pioneer Freighters listing his birth and death dates. Amasa Clark exemplified the independent spirit that has made the United States a great country.

Sarah Delany (1889–1999) and Bessie Delany (1891–1995)
African American Trailblazers

Self-reliant 106-year-old Sarah Delany, nicknamed "Sadie," and high-spirited 104-year-old Bessie Delany lived alone in their duplex home in New York for much of their adult lives. Refusing the modern-day intrusion of a telephone, the two ladies rigged a light to signal a neighbor in case of an emergency.

Old age created special problems for these two spinster sisters who stuck together for more than 80 years. The New York City Board of Education attempted to cut off Sadie's pension, forcing her to prove she was still alive at age 102.

An indomitable will and daily prayers, combined with a healthy lifestyle and strong genes, granted Sadie and Bessie more than 200 years of life. Avoiding tobacco, alcohol and fried foods, they consumed mainly vegetables, fruits and vitamins. A regimen of yoga and household chores provided the needed exercise. And they stayed away from probing and prying doctors. "They can kill you," Bessie used to say.[26]

The father of the Delany sisters had been born a slave in 1858. After emancipation, Henry Beard Delany, by dint of will, studied his way to become the first elected black bishop of the Episcopal Church, U.S.A., a source of pride to the entire family. Bishop Delany met his wife, Nanny Logan, at St. Augustine's School, where she graduated as the class valedictorian. Since Mama

Delany inherited fair skin from her white father, she could have elected to pass as a caucasian. However, she took pride in her black heritage and adored her dark-skinned husband.

Sadie, the second oldest of 10 Delany children, was born in Raleigh, Virginia, on September 19, 1889. Bessie, the third oldest, was born on September 3, 1891. Even as children, Sadie was the mama's child and Bessie the tough one. These roles continued into their adult years with Bessie taking enough chances for both of them. Throughout their days together, the sisters enjoyed a special bond based on their closeness in age and a feeling of mutual respect.

Suffering the indignities of the Jim Crow laws and the "separate but equal" ruling under the legal doctrine of *Plessy v. Ferguson,* Bishop Delany struggled to improve the opportunities for his children. Appearances became especially important. Every night, Mama Delany would bath her brood in a tin tub in reverse order of age, and each morning she'd line them up before school for Papa's inspection. Programmed for success by their role-model parents, all 10 Delany children completed college, continuing toward successful careers.

After graduating St. Augustine's, Sadie taught domestic science. Bessie also pursued teaching. Although both sisters were tall and extremely attractive with a choice of beaus, careers took precedence over their social life.

In 1916, Sadie Delany moved to New York to attend Pratt Institute. Bessie, sister Julia and brothers Hubert and Lucius joined her, all living in a sardine-can-sized apartment on 145th Street.

After two years at Pratt, Sadie transferred to Columbia Teacher's College, graduating in 1920. No matter how difficult the situation or how severe the bigotry aimed at a black southern woman in a white school, Sadie disassociated herself with a cool confidence, a legacy learned from her parents. A teacher described her thusly: "That Sarah Delany, you tell her to do something, she smiles at you, and then she just turns around and does what she wants."[27]

Bessie followed her sister to Columbia, attending its dental school after taking science courses at Shaw University in Raleigh. Brother Harry (Hap) already had graduated as a dentist from New York University, but the school refused women candidates.

Like her sister, Bessie suffered from intolerance. When a teacher gave Bessie's assignment a failing grade, a male friend presented it under his name. The assignment passed.

In 1923, Bessie Delany received a doctor of dental surgery degree. Her classmates elected her marshal at graduation, but she felt this was done so the white, male dentists could avoid marching beside her. Bessie hid her bitterness well. The caption under her picture in the Columbia yearbook read, "Bessie Delany, the perfect lady."

Dr. Bessie Delany shared an office with her brother Hap, a fellow dentist, and brother Lucius, an attorney. The second black female dentist in New York, Bessie collected the rent and handled the office books. Charging $2 for a cleaning, $2 for an extraction, $5 for a silver filling and $10 for gold, she maintained the same rates until her retirement. Her patients included Dr. Louis Wright, the chairman of the board of the National Association for the Advancement of Colored People. Hap treated entertainer Bojangles Robinson and Walter White of the NAACP. Twelve-hour days and caring for Mama at night following Papa's death crimped Sadie's and Bessie's dating. Neither ever married.

Sadie taught at PS 119 in Harlem and took speech lessons to soften her southern accent. She earned extra dollars selling candy to friends under the name "Delany's Delights." In 1925, she received a master's degree in education from Columbia. She continued to teach high school during the day and tutor adult dropouts during evenings until 1960. Sadie summarized her philosophy: "Life is short, and it's up to you to make it sweet."[28]

During the '30s and '40s, the sisters spent their free time watching baseball games or attending plays at the Bronx Opera House, while retaining a close relationship with their other eight siblings. This clean and wholesome lifestyle would have pleased Bishop Delany. When Sadie, even as an adult, dared to use the word "darn" in front of her mother, she received a strong verbal reprimand.

Bessie occasionally attended nightclubs with brother Hubert, an NAACP activist and assistant United States attorney for the southern district of New York, who lost a campaign for Congress before becoming a New York tax commissioner in 1934 and a justice of the Domestic Relations Court in 1942. Through Hubert, the sisters met entertainers Cab Calloway, Duke Ellington, Ethel Waters and William Kelly, editor of the *Amsterdam News* and a frequent houseguest.

Bessie actively fought prejudice whenever it reared its ugly head. She admired the brash strength of W. E. B. DuBois. Sadie leaned toward Booker T. Washington, a man who, like her father, sought advancement of blacks through education and civil obedience.

After Papa's death, Sadie accompanied Mama to Europe. A highlight of the trip involved a backstage visit with actor and civil rights activist Paul Robeson in London, following the production of *Othello*. Sister Bessie had known Paul from Columbia. Sadie and Mama went to the 1932 Olympics in Los Angeles, California, and visited Niagara Falls during another summer vacation.

Bessie's dental practice prevented extended travel, with the exception of a trip to Jamaica. The country's poverty appalled her, and she presented $2.50 gold pieces to the needy. Unfortunately, Bessie returned to Harlem with financial problems of her own. The depression had decimated her practice. It took years for her to get back on her feet. Luckily, Sadie's teaching salary and Mama's tiny pension saw them through the bad times.

As Mama reached 90, her declining physical skills demanded constant attention. Bessie retired from dentistry to provide full-time care for Mama. Sadie's teaching salary became the main support for the family. As a special treat for Mama, brother Hubert arranged for a private conference with Eleanor Roosevelt. Mama's excitement from the meeting stayed with her until the end of her days.

The onset of old age delivered sadness to the ladies. The death of so many friends and family members brought emptiness and loss. Brother Manross passed away first in 1955. Brother Lemuel and 95-year-old Mama died in 1956. Mama's passing affected Sadie the most. She moped around the house for months, unable to overcome her grief. Brother Sam, the baby of the brood, died in 1960. Brother Lucius passed away in 1969 and sister Julia in 1974 from an adverse reaction to penicillin.

However, the Delany sisters experienced the consolation of seeing an end to segregation and outliving the "Rebby boys," who had taunted them during their younger years.

Sadie and Bessie Delany lived simply. Their furniture came from the Salvation Army. The garden beside the house served as their greatest source of pride. Their failure to attend Martin Luther King's famous "I have a dream" speech in Washington, D.C., was among their greatest regrets.

Had either of the sisters become president, Bessie felt her first act would have been to outlaw taxes for anyone over 100. "They paid enough already."[29] Bessie felt certain her sister would go to heaven, but she questioned whether she would join her. "I'm just too mean."[30] However, the softening effect of more than 100 years just might have given her a chance.

With the years of experience came two books. Their first book, *Having Our Say,* besides becoming a best seller, was developed into a play that received three Tony nominations. Their second book was *The Delany Sisters' Book of Everyday Wisdom.*

On September 26, 1995, 104-year-old Dr. Bessie Delany died. Sadie fondly remembered her "baby sister" in the book *On My Own at 107: Reflections on Life without Bessie.* "I'm still kicking, just not as high," Sadie mused.

Sadie missed Bessie's mechanical skills around the house and her ability to study people almost as much as the day-to-day companionship. Although she thought about her sister constantly, Sadie Delany made it on her own until January 25, 1999, when she died at age 109.

Through a combination of grit and determination, the Delany sisters bested adversity and discrimination, becoming role models in the creation of modest, moderate and meaningful centenarian lives.

Marjory Stoneman Douglas (1890–1998)
Author and Environmentalist

Young Marjory Stoneman Douglas's early years gave little hint of her future greatness as an author and speaker on environmental issues. Born in Minneapolis, Minnesota, on April 7, 1890, to Lillian Trefethen, who barely stood five feet tall, and Frank Stoneman, Marjory weighed a roly-poly 12 pounds at birth. An unattractive and pudgy infant, she grew into a fat child with a crossed left eye and sought companionship in picture books.

As an only offspring, Marjory became the center of attention of her parents and grandparents. Unfortunately, her father had difficulty earning a living in a building and loan company and moved the family to Providence, near his wife's parents. As Mr. Stoneman's business troubles continued to magnify, Lillian's mental health collapsed, causing her daughter to become further withdrawn and introverted. Lillian was taken to a sanitarium and returned home beaten and subdued, and Marjory found herself the six-year-old "mother" of a mother-child.

Marjory's father, feeling trapped by his wife's mental incapacity and his own economic failure, abandoned his family and fled to Florida. He never contributed to his daughter's upbringing nor made an effort to communicate with her. With nowhere else to go, Lillian and her daughter moved in with her parents, the Trefethens, who were tiny people who lived contained lives. Grandpa had no close friends because he believed "close friends would only cheat you."[31] Although uncommunicative and moody, Mr. Trefethen was a good person who eked out a living in a foundry, sharing what he could with his granddaughter and daughter.

Marjory loved to read, write, think and create. At age nine, she invented a puzzle called "Double the Headings and Curtailings," which *St. Nicholas Magazine* published.

As a child from a broken home, Marjory Stoneman developed the outlook of a skeptic and dissenter, much like the Quakers on her father's side of the family. Although she was confirmed as an Episcopalian, "church never struck her as making good sense."[32]

Marjory's school life saddened as she grew older. In high school she was the fat girl who wore glasses and had long stringy hair. The boys never asked her to dance at cotillions, so she became a wallflower who hid her loneliness in books. However, Marjory's classmates respected her ability with words, nominating her to write the "Parting Ode" for the graduating class.

Marjory attended college at Wellesley, only one and one-half hours from her home, to be near her mother. Since she received straight As in high school, her teachers allowed her to register for advanced English. As an added benefit at Wellesley, her wandering eye suddenly corrected itself, and she no longer needed glasses. Underdeveloped in the ways of the world yet intellectually mature, Marjory found Wellesley to be the perfect institution to nourish her mind while guarding her virginity.

During her junior year, Marjory's mother developed breast cancer, causing her to become even more fearful and childlike. Lillian Stoneman's death the week of her daughter's graduation caused an already overburdened Marjory terrible anguish.

Overcoming her sorrow, the newly graduated Marjory got a job at a Bamberger's department store in Trenton, New Jersey, at $20 per week. She frequently visited the library across the street, seeking the companionship of books. By accident, she met Kenneth Douglas, a social service editor for the *Newark Evening News,* who was nearly 30 years her senior. Kenneth's attention caused new and wonderful sensations to surge through her body. Within three months, Kenneth and she were married. Marjory reveled in the joys of marriage and sex, a new experience for this young woman who had been taught to hold a tight rein on her emotions.

Marjory knew almost nothing about her husband other than that he made her happy. One day a policeman knocked on their apartment door and arrested Kenneth for passing a bad check. Found guilty, he served six months in the penitentiary.

After being released, Kenneth wrote Marjory's father in Florida in an attempt to bilk him out of some money. Although Marjory's marriage, which she treated as a glorious adventure, ended in divorce, she had no regrets. Inadvertently, her husband had reunited her with her father, who had sent his brother to New Jersey to determine the identity of this Kenneth Douglas and why he wanted money.

Marjory's father invited her to join him in Florida, and the two saw each other for the first time since she was six years old. She instantly forgave him for his years of isolation, happy to have a father once again. Mr. Stoneman at last had achieved financial success. After abandoning his family in Providence, he worked at a variety of jobs until he scraped together enough money to invest in a small morning newspaper. To add to his happiness, Frank Stoneman had remarried a wonderful woman, who happened to be a direct descendant of President Thomas Jefferson.

Frank Stoneman also had passed the Florida bar exam and even won an election for a circuit judgeship. Governor Napoleon Bonaparte Broward, a political enemy who viewed Mr. Stoneman and his newspaper as direct opposition to his dream of an expanding industrial base throughout southern Florida, refused to sign the document allowing him to serve on the bench. Rather than pursue the judgeship, Mr. Stoneman concentrated his efforts on his morning paper, the *Miami News Record,* which supported a bill to protect the Everglades against land speculators and almost certainly gave birth to his daughter's pro-ecology views.

In 1910, the *News Record* became the *Miami Herald.* Hired by her father as a reporter, Marjory loved her work, eventually rising to society editor. Her father and she developed an intellectual kinship and mutual respect for each other's skills. He taught her the cardinal rule of newspaper reporting: "Get your facts straight."[33] She taught him the importance of total commitment.

While writing a story on the first woman to enlist in any branch of the service during World War I, the impetuous Marjory decided to become that first woman to enlist in the Navy Reserves. The Navy made her a yeoman first class, and she spent the most boring year of her life issuing boat licenses. Hating the humdrum routine, she begged her commandant to grant her a discharge. When he agreed, she joined the American Red Cross in France.

At the war's end, Majory Douglas accompanied a Red Cross shipment of corrugated iron barracks for the unfortunate victims of an earthquake outside Florence, Italy. Somehow the shipment mysteriously disappeared along with her wallet and money.

When Marjory joined a Red Cross camera crew sent to the Balkans to survey the results of the war in that part of the world, she met a young man named Frederick. The couple's friendship blossomed in that strange and romantic setting. Frederick and Marjory became engaged in a whirlwind courtship. When Marjory returned to the United States with her fiancé, she realized that she did not love Frederick enough to marry him and broke off the engagement.

After a brief visit with her 94-year-old grandfather in Providence, Marjory returned to the normalcy of Florida and the job of assistant editor of the *Miami Herald* under her father.

Although Marjory dated from time to time, she decided she was "not the marrying kind." She chose to live as an individual and gave up on romance.

Once back in Miami, Marjory increased her commitment to the Everglades. She had become friends with Ruth Bryan Owens, the daughter of William Jennings Bryan, once secretary of state under President Woodrow Wilson. Ruth Owens became the first woman to represent Florida in Congress and an ardent protector of the Everglades.

Ernest Coe, a landscape architect who lost his money in Florida real estate speculation, had initiated the idea for an Everglades park. Coe talked Ruth and Marjory into serving on his committee.

Marjory involved herself diligently on the Everglades project in addition to a variety of local charities. Her long hours at the paper and a natural propensity to be overly emotional added to an overall feeling of mental and physical fatigue. "I would black out while speaking to a friend, suddenly become rigid, blank as if a shutter had been drawn over my mind."[34]

Marjory's doctor cautioned her to resign from the paper to stem the stress. Accepting the medical advice, she quit to write short stories. Although her father had counted on his daughter's eventually taking over the paper, he supported her decision to resign.

Marjory sold one-line aphorisms to magazines while working on a novella called *White Midnight,* for which she eventually received $600. Her romantic short stories could be found in the *Saturday Evening Post* and *Ladies Home Journal.* Although her grandmother would raise herself to her full five feet and disapprovingly point her finger at Marjory and threaten, "You will die in a garret," Marjory continued to pour out a string of fiction.[35]

Marjory Stoneman Douglas, then 34, still lived with her father and his wife. Recognizing a need for greater independence, she oversaw the building of a tiny house in Coconut Grove, one of the best decisions she felt she had ever made. She relished her privacy and loved to tinker around the house when she was not writing or reading.

In 1940, Marjory's father died at the age of 84 due to complications from a kidney stone. Just the year before, he had traveled to Europe with the Carnegie Foundation for Peace to meet various European heads of state and lecture at Westminster Abbey in London. Her father's death triggered another psychological attack, forcing her to seek medical help.

Once Marjory recovered, Hervey Allen, the author of the popular novel *Anthony Adverse* and editor of a rivers of America series for Rinehart and Company, commissioned her to write a book on the Miami River. Based on her familiarity with southern Florida and a writer's whim, she countered with a project on the Everglades, which Allen accepted. After receiving a $1,000 advance, she spent nearly five years in research. In 1947, *The Everglades: River of Grass* was published, coinciding with the founding of the Everglades National Park. The book became an immediate success and an important cog in the ecological movement.

As Marjory aged, she carefully paced herself. She danced and swam for exercise until well into her 70s. She never drove a car, believing it wasn't worth the effort. Although she enjoyed an occasional Sazerac or scotch, Marjory rarely overdid anything.

Marjory's writing continued to keep her mind busy. In 1952, she penned *Road to the Sun,* a didactic story about people caught up in a land boom on the edge of the Everglades. *Freedom River* and *Alligator Crossing,* two novels set in southern Florida, followed during the late '50s.

Marjory's health derived from a combination of good genes— both of her mother's parents lived well into their '90s—a sensible lifestyle, a low-fat diet of little meat and lots of fish and vegetables, two aspirins a day to thin her blood, moderate exercise and lots of luck. She believed her ability to relax played a prominent role in her longevity. At the age of 70, her appendix burst and she almost died of peritonitis, forcing her to spend one month in the hospital battling the poisons pouring through her body.

After her release from the hospital, the University of Miami Press appointed Marjory to serve on its advisory board. She also lectured on Florida history at Dade Junior College. She would stand and speak to her class for two hours at a time. At the end of the period, she often felt more energized than tired.

Since *River of Grass* had sold well, Harper and Row hired Marjory to write a book entitled *Florida: The Long Frontier,* which was published in 1967.

A friend, Dr. Frank Chapman, an expert on the English writer W. H. Hudson, believing himself too old to complete a biography on the author, urged Marjory to complete the project. Marjory took Dr. Chapman's reference notes and used a grant from Wellesley to develop a book. Her research took her on several trips to Argentina, where Hudson had spent several years, and England, where he had done most of his writing. Since deterioration of the retina had caused her eyesight to fail, she required a secretary's assistance. She would spend much of 19 years on this work.

As Marjory Douglas entered her 80th year, she concentrated her energy on the preservation of the Everglades. Most of her family had died, and she felt alone. She needed to channel her vitality and intensity into a meaningful cause. When she praised a member of the Audubon Society at a grocery store on her work on behalf of the Everglades, the member looked her straight in the eye and said, "Yeah, what are you doing?"

"Oh me, I wrote the book," Marjory bristled, surprised by the comment.

"That's not enough," countered the Audubon Society member. "We need people to help."[36]

Thus motivated, Marjory founded the Friends of the Everglades, on whose behalf she raised thousands of dollars and made speeches fighting all efforts to "drain, plug, stanch, dike and otherwise remove water from the Everglades."[37]

Age and illness might have stolen her vision but they could not still her voice. "Sight isn't everything in the world. The worst thing is to die young. Eat right and have the right attitude. If you neglect your brain, it will deteriorate. Continue to be interested in new ideas. Stretch your mind," she advised those around her.[38]

Philosophically, Marjory considered herself an agnostic, a doubter, who had difficulty accepting the concept of a soul. Yet she believed in a single universe. "Life has been plenty. I believe it should be lived so vividly that thoughts of another life are not necessary."[39]

In 1991, Queen Elizabeth, an ardent conservationist who admired Marjory's skill as a speaker and writer, congratulated Mrs. Douglas on her dedication to the Everglades. Two years later, President Clinton awarded her the Presidential Medal of Honor. President Clinton said, "Long before there was an Earth Day, Mrs. Douglas was a passionate steward of our nation's natural resources, particularly her Florida Everglades."[40]

When asked on her 100th birthday if she had hopes for the survival of the Everglades, Marjory answered, "I am neither an optimist or a pessimist. I say it's got to be done."[41]

Marjory Stoneman Douglas died at home on May 14, 1998, at the age of 108. After her cremation, her ashes were scattered over a portion of the Everglades National Park that bore her name, a fitting honor for one who had dedicated herself to the preservation of the Florida environment.

Eleanor Lansing Dulles (1895–1996)
Author, Educator and United States Diplomat

Born in Watertown, New York, in 1895, the fourth child of Presbyterian minister Allen Macy Dulles and Edith Foster Dulles, Eleanor Lansing Dulles grew up happy and carefree. She also developed the independent spirit of a girl raised with two older brothers who teased her mercilessly.

Her mother named her in honor of her sister, Eleanor Foster Lansing, the wife of Robert Lansing, who would serve as President Wilson's secretary of state. As a child, Eleanor spent hours chatting with her great-grandmother, a Civil War widow who lived to be 96, and her grandfather, General John Foster, the secretary of state under President Benjamin Harrison, who enthralled her with stories of Mexico, Russia and Spain.

The young girl with the thick-rimmed glasses would escape to distant lands through the books in the house's large library. A string of writers ran through the Dulles family. Grandfather John Dulles had written *Life in India,* describing his years in the ministry. Grandfather John Foster had written *Diplomatic Memoirs,* and her father had authored *The True Church.* Eleanor would hone her own writing skills through the years. She also enjoyed outdoor activities, especially swimming and fishing in the lake near her home.

Father, a Princeton graduate and an intellectual, concentrated on spirituality. Mother handled the family's executive responsibilities. Although only five foot five, Mother Dulles stood tall in household matters.

The five Dulles children were an amazing lot. John Foster Dulles, the oldest brother, born in 1888, became Eleanor's lifelong role model. Sister Margaret followed the next year. Brother Allen, born three years later, a future director of the CIA (Central Intelligence Agency), required surgery to correct a club foot. Eleanor was born in 1895, and sister Nataline completed the Dulles family in 1898.

Brother Allen wrote *The Boer War* when he was just eight years old. Grandfather Foster published the book, which sold more than 4,000 copies, an accomplishment recognized by the *New York Times*. Brother Foster graduated from Princeton as valedictorian, earning a $600 prize for his excellence in philosophy.

Eleanor had difficulty meeting the high scholastic standards set by her older brothers. She struggled with an innate shyness, compensating with a hearty handshake and a strong determination to succeed. She won the New England Scholarship to Bryn Mawr College in 1914, achieving the first of her 11 earned and honorary degrees.

Eleanor's educational career at Bryn Mawr proved mediocre. Like "flotsam and jetsam," she floated from subject to subject without concentrating. On one theme her teacher wrote, "This is an absurd attempt to cover the ridiculous with nonsense."[42] Such criticism deeply hurt her.

After failing a chemistry examination, Eleanor gave up hope for a career in medicine. However, she excelled in the rest of her studies and starred on the college swimming, water polo and field polo teams, where the girls nicknamed her "Dooles."

With the start of World War I and her graduation from Bryn Mawr, Eleanor Dulles wished to do her part for the war effort. She sailed to France to aid displaced refugees. A family gift of $1,000 provided her with the necessary expense money. She arranged for canned goods for the undernourished, medicine for the sick and housing for the homeless, applying limited resources to massive human distress.

After the armistice, her brother Foster assisted the world-renowned economist John Maynard Keynes to develop scenarios on financial restitution, largely through the influence of his "Uncle Bert," the United States Secretary of State Robert Lansing. Brother Allen, a government employee, helped formulate new boundary lines for Germany. With her own work on displaced refugees completed, Eleanor traveled to the Marne region of France, where the devastation caused by the war staggered her.

A few weeks later, an older and more experienced Eleanor returned to the United States sporting a short haircut and silk stockings, smoking Fatimas and spicing her vocabulary with an occasional "damn." An unexpected offer of a fellowship from Bryn Mawr led to a master's degree in social economy.

Although the Dulles family had a distinguished pedigree, attended the correct colleges and knew the proper people, Eleanor's parents were not rich, and she had to earn her own living. Following a brief stay with the American Tube and Stamping Company, Eleanor found employment in the payroll department of a hairnet factory at $18 per week. An increase to $25 per week and a strong savings ethic created a nest egg of $800. Aching with ideas and determined to attain a doctorate, Eleanor enrolled at the London School of Economics in England. She went on to receive her second master's degree from Harvard in 1924.

The next year, Eleanor Dulles returned to France for research on a doctoral thesis concerning the French franc, using funds provided by the Bureau of International Research. Her monumental book *The French Franc* theorized that psychology and politics determine the velocity of the circulation of money. After returning to the United States, she received her doctorate in economics from Harvard and Radcliffe.

Eleanor went back to her beloved Paris to research a book on international settlements for Radcliffe and Harvard. There she met David Blondheim, a previously married Jew with a son. He was 41, she 30. David had little hair, wore thick glasses like hers, stood barely taller than she, but was blessed with sensitive eyes and a sturdy body. A keen conversationalist with a quick wit and a love of books, he spoke fluent French, Hebrew, German, Italian and Spanish. David quickly developed into Eleanor's friend and soul mate.

As her love blossomed, Eleanor recognized the growing anti-Semitism in Germany. Brother Foster attempted to calm her fears by calling this distasteful part of Nazism "a passing phase," but Eleanor knew better.[43]

After the death of her father in 1931, Eleanor married David against the wishes of both families. She had been teaching at Bryn Mawr and the University of Pennsylvania, while completing her book *Depression and Reconstruction*. David taught at Johns Hopkins University. The marriage became a commuter's nightmare. She lived in Philadelphia, maintaining her maiden name for professional reasons, and he in Baltimore. Only on holidays and weekends would the two intellectuals meet in one or the other city.

Although the couple experienced financial problems, David made Eleanor happy. Unfortunately, David Blondheim's obsession with the religion he had abandoned caused him an all-pervading sadness. In March 1934, after less than two years of marriage, Eleanor told her husband she was pregnant. Depressed with fathering a son outside his faith, David placed his head in a gas oven and committed suicide. Eleanor gave birth to a son, David Dulles, seven months after her husband's death.

David Blondheim's suicide toughened Eleanor. She refused to allow life to defeat her. When the newly designated Social Security Board offered her a position in 1936, she gladly accepted. Senator Arthur Vandenberg, an enemy of the Roosevelt administration, attempted to abolish the agency, but Eleanor reassured his committee on the sufficiency of the size, character and disposition of the Social Security agency's reserves. Based on the arguments she presented, the senator withdrew his objections.

Since Eleanor always had wanted two children, she adopted Ann Welsh Dulles in February 1937. A housekeeper helped her balance motherhood with a busy career.

In 1938, the Social Security Administration sent Eleanor Dulles to Geneva as the conference representative on social insurance payments. Shortly after the start of World War II, she transferred to the Board Of Economic Welfare, a dead-end job.

Eleanor Dulles finally made her mark in the State Department. She spent several months on the United Nations Relief and Rehabilitation Administration issue, attending the International Monetary Conference in Bretton Woods, New Hampshire.

The years of loneliness after David's death and her frustration with "being a woman in a man's world" left her open for an affair with a Russian emigré. Philosophical and political differences eventually led to a separation, and she immersed herself in her family and work.

The mid-'40s gained Eleanor an appointment to the State Department's "German Committee." Visiting Berlin, she witnessed the horrible destruction caused by the Allied bombs. Her primary responsibility centered on the economic recovery of postwar Austria. She worked miracles to return the country to normalcy, bartering Lippizaner horses in exchange for cabbages and potatoes to feed the hungry masses.

Capitalizing on her political connections, Eleanor Dulles obtained more than $1 million in needed Marshall Plan aid to erect schools, factories and housing throughout Austria. She spent her weekends visiting her children in Switzerland, a safe haven for civilian dependents. In 1948, after Eleanor had helped pull Austria back to its feet, an appreciative Chancellor Leopold Figl hosted a farewell banquet in her honor.

The expertise of Eleanor on German affairs led to her promotion to the "Berlin Desk," designed to assist the demolished city's reconstruction. The job combined the ideal assortment of excitement and difficulty. Her previous experience in Austria had provided the perfect training ground.

The United States struggled to make Berlin into an island of freedom in a red sea of Communism. Eleanor Dulles, aptly named "The Mother of Berlin," labored to develop the city into a showplace.

When Eleanor arrived in Germany, Berlin was suffering an unemployment rate of nearly 33 percent. She was determined to rehabilitate the city. While commuting between Washington and Berlin, she secured more than $1 billion in American funds to rebuild demolished areas and create a stockpile of supplies in case of a Communist blockade. "Little by little, like corals building a reef, I built a situation in Berlin," Eleanor boasted.[44] Her brother Foster, upon being named secretary of state by President Dwight Eisenhower, asked her to resign from her "man's job" to avoid any hint of nepotism. Eleanor staunchly refused.

Eleanor's enthusiasm delivered positive economic results. New hospitals and entertainment centers sprouted throughout Berlin. The erection of Congress Hall proved to be her crowning achievement. Nicknamed the "Pregnant Oyster" and "Frau Dulles's Hut," the building became a city center for meetings and recreation. A grateful President Eisenhower eventually recognized the importance of Eleanor's work by granting her the permanent rank of minister.

Thanksgiving of 1958 in McLean, Virginia, would be the last holiday Allen, Foster and Eleanor Dulles spent together as a family. After a relaxed lunch featuring a martini toast, the phone rang to summon the three siblings to their offices. Premier Krushchev of Russia had vowed to liberate Berlin from the Americans, creating a potential international explosion. Following coffee and a final brandy, Foster returned to the State Department to work on policy, Allen to the CIA to answer the charge that Berlin had become a hotbed of espionage and Eleanor to write a series of press releases. The Dulleses would be at their respective desks by three in the afternoon.

On May 24, 1959, John Foster Dulles, a man Eleanor both jealously loved and respected, died of cancer after a long and valiant battle. Events in Eleanor's life deteriorated rapidly. Although she had achieved her position in the State Department on her own merits, her superiors transferred her to the Bureau of Intelligence and Research, an expected yet unwelcome change after a three-year stint at the Berlin Desk. With more spare time available she researched a book about her Berlin years, *The Wall Is Not Forever*. A gallbladder operation at the end of 1959 ended this difficult year in Eleanor's life.

During the early '60s she visited 47 different countries over a three-year period for the State Department. One of her most memorable experiences included a private interview with Generalissimo Chiang Kai-shek and his wife, a future centenarian.

Madame Chiang's shrewd translation of her husband's comments and control of the meeting left a lasting impression on Eleanor.

To maintain her fitness, Eleanor swam during her free time. However, the gallstones remaining in her system following her earlier surgery caused her continual discomfort. In Nepal, a missionary advised her to seek immediate medical attention, but she ignored the advice. Fighting off the pain, she continued to Pakistan, Iran and Paris before returning to Boston to spend her 66th birthday at the Leahy Clinic to remove the gallstones. While recovering in the hospital, Bryn Mawr bestowed a citation upon her for her work as a "Diplomat and Economist."

The John Kennedy family placed much of the responsibility for the failure of the American-sponsored attack on Cuba at the Bay of Pigs on the shoulders of the director of the CIA, Allen Dulles, forcing his resignation. Eleanor's strong opinions had created her own share of political enemies. A few months after Allen's departure, Secretary of State Dean Rusk summoned her and said, "The White House has asked me to get rid of you."[45] Eleanor Dulles carried her books down the corridor to the elevator and unceremoniously loaded them into a friend's station wagon.

Now considered a pariah by the Kennedy establishment, Eleanor Dulles visited Latin America as a private citizen and lectured throughout the United States to earn money.

Through the intercession of an old State Department friend, Ambassador George Allen, a Duke University board member, Eleanor obtained a temporary teaching assignment at the school. In addition, Harcourt Brace provided her an advance for a book on her brother John Foster Dulles. During the summer of 1962, she reminisced with President Eisenhower in his study at Gettysburg about her brother. Eisenhower called his relationship with Foster an "ideal combination."[46] In fact, the president offered him a seat on the Supreme Court following Chief Justice Frederick Vinson's death, but Foster refused, believing he would be more useful in his role as secretary of state.

Eleanor Dulles accepted a full-time academic position at Georgetown University, where she worked for the next seven years. In 1964, the first of two retina reattachments interrupted her teaching.

In 1965, the German government honored her on her 70th birthday, and the Washington embassy presented her with a silver tray engraved with the names of 14 old friends.

Unwilling to slow down, Eleanor Dulles wrote *One Germany or Two: The Struggle at the Heart of Europe* and *American Foreign Policy in the Making* during the late '60s. In 1967, she served as an official state representative along with President Lyndon Johnson at the funeral of West Germany's Chancellor Konrad Adenauer.

Throughout the '70s, Eleanor traveled extensively. She visited Soviet Russia to view firsthand "the deadening effect of dictatorship and the loss of inspiration that comes with a Communist regime."[47]

Although several cataract operations slowed her progress, she visited China in 1979 against her ophthalmologist's advice. She felt she had to feel the pulse of such a great and growing nation.

Although men had seized the leadership roles throughout her life, Eleanor Dulles struggled to create her own niche. With two famous brothers, she earned her own intellectual independence, not from a spirit of hostility, but with a firm commitment to improve the world around her, a task she executed to the fullest. Some might have considered Eleanor an irritant, but she charged forward with the unwavering faith of one who believed in what she did.

Eleanor retained her indomitable will until the end. Her nieces, nephews, children and six grandchildren provided her greatest joy and remembrances. Suffering from diminished eyesight and failed hearing, Eleanor Lansing Dulles died at the Knollwood Military Retirement Home at the age of 101 on October 30, 1996. Her diplomatic and academic achievements combined with her successes in reconstructing a bombed-out Berlin to make her one of the outstanding women of the 20th century.

Hamilton Fish (1888–1991)
United States Congressman

Hamilton Fish, whose lineage included a congressman father and a grandfather who had been secretary of state to President Ulysses Grant, viewed himself as a direct extension of his family linkage to politics. He was born on December 7, 1888, in Garrison, New York, within view of the United States Military Academy.

Fish's mother, whose father and brother both had been mayors of Troy, New York, died before Hamilton's 11th birthday. In 1896, he attended a Swiss school near Geneva, where he learned to climb mountains, speak French and play soccer. He graduated high school from the exclusive St. Marks School in Massachusetts. Although a good student, Fish excelled at athletics, especially football.

In 1906, the six-foot, four-inch, 200-pounder enrolled at Harvard, where he starred as a tackle, twice being selected to Walter Camp's All-American football team. The Crimson 11 won the national championship, defeating Jim Thorpe's Carlisle College team by the score of 17 to 0. Fish acted as captain for the game. He eventually would be enshrined in the College Football Hall of Fame in South Bend, Indiana.

In addition to participating in athletics, Fish served as president of Harvard's Hasty Pudding Club and graduated cum laude at the age of 20. His classmates included poet T. S. Eliot; Brigadier

General Theodore Roosevelt, Jr.; Jack Reed, author of *Ten Days That Shook the World;* and newspaper reporter Walter Lippmann.

Fish turned down an offer to teach history at his alma mater so that he could work with an insurance agency. However, his family background ensured an interest in politics. He attended the Republican National Convention with his father in 1912, when Roosevelt bolted the GOP to form the Bull Moose Party. Fish parlayed a chairmanship of the Putnam County Bull Moose Party to a seat in the New York state assembly.

Hamilton enlisted in the army during World War I, serving as a captain in an all-black regiment, the famed "Harlem Hellfighters." At the Battle of Meuse-Argonne, he received the silver star for bravery under fire and was inducted into the French Legion of Honor.

After returning to the states at the war's end, Hamilton Fish married Grace Chapin, a widow with two tiny children whose father had been a congressman. In short order, the citizens of Hyde Park elected the returning war hero with the political pedigree to the United States House of Representatives.

Congressman Fish initiated a chain of legislation. He introduced a resolution calling for the return of the body of the unknown soldier from Europe to Arlington National Cemetery and sponsored a bill to erect a monument for the black soldiers who had served in the war. Violently isolationist, Fish called for a committee to investigate Communist activities in the United States. He opposed Franklin Roosevelt's attempt to pack the Supreme Court with 15 justices when its 9 members declared the president's effort to regulate prices and wages to be unconstitutional, fueling a growing enmity between the two Harvard graduates from Hyde Park.

As the ranking Republican of the House Committee on Foreign Affairs, Fish opposed the United States' involvement in World War II. He had experienced the hell of World War I, and he fought to maintain his country's neutrality.

"It is none of our business what form of government may exist in Soviet Russia, Fascist Italy, Imperial Japan or Nazi Germany, any more than it is their business what form of government exists in our own country. We have our own problems to solve in America without being involved in the rotten mess in Europe," Fish told the press.[48]

Fish believed Franklin Roosevelt had antagonized and manipulated the Axis nations. Fearing the tragic effects of war, he proposed a 30-day moratorium at the Oslo Conference in 1939 to allow adequate time for the settlement of international disputes by arbitration and mediation. When Great Britain objected, Fish withdrew the resolution, fearing the worst. Within two weeks, war exploded throughout Europe.

During the 1940 presidential campaign, Roosevelt denounced Fish and two other isolationists, Representative Joseph Martin of Massachusetts and Senator Bruce Barton of Connecticut, as "Martin, Barton and Fish." The cadence of the three names could be heard across the country as a sign of reproach.

Following the Japanese attack on Pearl Harbor, which Fish felt had been manipulated by the bullying tactics of Roosevelt and his hired henchman, Harry Dexter White, the congressman patriotically supported the war effort.

Fish continued his verbal attack on the president. What the United States gained on the battlefield, Roosevelt lost at the conference table. Duped by Russia at Tehran and Yalta, Roosevelt had ceded too much to Joseph Stalin and Communist Russia. He had betrayed the people of Poland, who had placed their hopes in freedom and democracy.

With the cessation of hostilities, Congressman Fish proposed several bills calling for food relief in the occupied countries. He introduced a resolution in Congress denouncing Adolph Hitler for the murder of millions of Jews and condemned the English for their de facto repudiation of the Balfour Declaration, which supported a Jewish homeland.

Congressman Fish lost a bid for re-election in 1944. His old enemy Franklin Roosevelt combined forces with Thomas Dewey to redistrict Fish out of three Republican counties. His refusal to adopt a conciliatory attitude with the Republican leadership made Fish a party outsider. Although he would serve as a Republican committeeman from Newburgh, he never would win another elected political office.

Fish returned to the insurance business for several years prior to purchasing the anti-Communist magazine *Today's World—The*

Magazine That Dares to Tell The Truth. He frequently wrote under the pseudonym Junius Americanus, much like the 18th-century American patriots who assumed Latin names.

Throughout his life, Fish railed against the evils of Communism. In 1946, he wrote *The Challenge of World Communism.* He voiced a progressive civil rights agenda combined with a policy of avoiding international entanglements. He claimed to be a friend of Israel and all democratic countries throughout the world.

After his wife, Grace, died in 1960, Fish continued lecturing and writing. He strongly opposed the entry of the United States into the Communist cesspool in Vietnam.

In 1969, Fish's son ran for and won a Republican seat in the United States House of Representatives. The next year the proud father found love again and married a Russian emigré, Marie Choubaroff Blackton, who loved to speak French with her husband. Marie died of cancer in 1974.

Fish's political views eventually created a rift between him and his son. When Congressman Hamilton Fish Jr. voted to impeach Richard Nixon, his father placed ads in the local newspapers supporting the president. When his grandson, Hamilton Fish III, a Democrat and publisher of the leftist magazine *The Nation,* ran for Congress in 1988, Fish denounced him.

In 1976, Hamilton Fish married Alice Curtis Desmond, a wealthy descendant of William Bradford, a 17th century governor of Massachusetts. Alice Desmond had written 22 books, and in 1980, the couple financed the Alice Desmond and Hamilton Fish Library in Garrison, New York, the repository of both families' papers.

The marriage proved tumultuous. Alice had a sensitive and creative nature. Fish displayed the strong opinions that made him either loved or hated by those who knew him. He dressed carelessly, she meticulously. Hamilton frequently forgot his wife's birthday or their anniversary. In 1984, Alice divorced him.

In 1988, Fish married for a fourth time. The 99-year-old and his new wife, Lydia Ambogio, a journalist, appeared on Charles Kuralt's *Sunday Morning* television show. During the year, Fish also delivered a speech against nuclear arms proliferation.

Hamilton Fish continued to remain active—writing, speaking and attending political rallies—until two weeks before his death. Rarely sick, Fish never smoked and drank alcohol sparingly. He frequently walked for exercise and rarely watched television other than sports. Until late in life he attended the Harvard-Yale football game.

Hamilton Fish died on January 18, 1991, at his home in Cold Spring, New York, at the age of 102. A crowd of more than 700 filled the cadet chapel at West Point for his memorial service. After the congregation sang "God Bless America," Congressman Hamilton Fish Jr. and Secretary of the Army Michael Stone delivered eulogies. The old warrior was buried with full military honors at St. Philips Episcopal Church in Garrison.

Madame (Mai-Ling Soong) Chiang Kai-Shek (1897–   )
Author and Diplomat

The Soong family myth begins in 1885, when nine-year-old Charlie Soong was sent by his parents in China to an uncle in Massachusetts to protect him from the turmoil of the Taiping Rebellion.

The everyday drudgery of working in his uncle's rice store bored the ambitious boy. Seeking to improve his lot, the youth escaped to stow away on a ship anchored in the Boston Harbor. The ship's captain, Charles Jones, took an instant liking to his new cabin boy. After the captain urged him to convert to Christianity, "Charles Jones" Soong adopted his patron's name as his own. His new church provided a scholarship to Trinity College, later renamed Duke University. As he struggled to master the intricacies of the English language, Charlie joked, "I'd rudder be Soong den too late."[49] His charm and wit made him popular with his classmates.

After transferring to Vanderbilt and graduating with honors, a thoroughly Americanized Charlie Soong returned to China to the unfamiliar sights and smells of plum sauce, spices and flowers intermingled with the pungent stench of masses of humanity. A stranger in a strange land, he studied the Shanghai dialect to acquire the necessary linguistic skills to serve as an itinerant minister in his native country.

In 1887, Charlie Soong wed a 19-year-old educated Chinese girl who would provide him with five children. Success came quickly to the diminutive entrepreneur and his wife. He resigned from the ministry to earn a fortune selling Bibles and also formed a profitable noodle-brokerage business. As China's monarchy weakened, Soong dabbled in the anti-Manchu dynasty revolutionary movement along with the legendary Dr. Sun Yat-sen, a fellow churchgoer and a lifelong friend.

Soong's wife gave birth to daughter Ai-ling in 1890. Daughter Ching-ling followed in 1892 and son T. V. in 1894. Pudgy Mai-ling, whose name translated to "beautiful mood," was born on February 12, 1897. Brothers TL and TA completed the Soong family.

Mai-ling ruled the Soong household with a child's iron hand. Nicknamed "Little Lantern" by her fellow siblings for her girth, she idolized her oldest sister, Ai-ling. After begging to be sent at age five to the McTyeire School, one of the country's finest preparatory institutions, just like Ai-ling, Mai-ling suffered nightmares and had to return home. This minor setback had little effect on Mai-ling's future as a student or a woman of the world.

Charlie Soong recognized how important an American college education might be for his children. He sent Ai-ling to Wesleyan College in Macon, Georgia. A few years later, Mai-ling and Ching-ling attended school in Summit, New Jersey, prior to joining Ai-ling at Wesleyan. Too young to go to college, precocious Mai-ling received special tutoring. With lots of free time on her hands, the mischievous Mai-ling frequently found herself in trouble with her teachers for one tiny indiscretion after another, but she possessed the gift of talking her way out of punishment.

While Mai-ling spent her carefree years in school, vast changes permeated the Chinese landscape. The Empress Dowager had died in 1908 after almost one-half century of rule. Revolution and anarchy vied to fill the power void. With the Manchu leadership ended, Sun Yat-sen formed the Kuomintang Nationalist Party (KMT), which sought a democratic revolution of the people, and rose to become provisional president of the Republic of China in Nanjing.

After a grown-up Ai-ling Soong returned to China following her education in the states, a still-married, middle-aged Dr. Sun became smitten with his best friend's daughter. When he proposed marriage, a horrified Charlie Soong ordered his friend to leave the house. "My door is closed to you forever."[50]

However, Charlie Soong forgave the affront and opted to support Dr. Sun's movement. When revolution again erupted, Dr. Sun fled to Japan. The Soong family followed, and Ai-ling served as secretary to the ousted president.

In 1913, Ai-ling married the prestigious H. H. Kung, a direct descendant of Confucius and an Oberlin- and Yale-educated financial genius. Ching-ling replaced her sister as secretary to Dr. Sun. He was nearly 50, she only 20. Although the Soong family had arranged Ching-ling's engagement to a young man from a good family, she fell in love with Dr. Sun. When Charlie tried to separate Ching-ling from Dr. Sun, his daughter climbed out her bedroom window and sailed to Kobe into her lover's arms. Dr. Sun divorced his wife of many years and married Ching-ling.

Charlie Soong sought to retrieve Ching-ling prior to the ceremony but arrived too late. Disowning her, the disconsolate father bemoaned the loss of both his daughter and his best friend.

Meanwhile, Mai-ling transferred from Wesleyan College to Wellesley in Boston to be close to brother T. V., who was a Harvard student. Like a caterpillar transformed into a butterfly, the chubby teenage girl turned into a graceful and beautiful woman with large, almond-shaped, penetrating eyes. Majoring in English, Mai-ling engrossed herself in the myth and magic of the Arthurian legends while sharpening her writing skills.

In 1918, Charlie Soong died from cancer. Some say he died of a broken heart because of his daughter's disobedience. Others believed he succumbed to poison administered by his enemies.

Ai-ling, as her father's political successor, allied herself with Shanghai's notorious "Green Gang," an unsavory ring led by a big-eared tough named Tu. A young, ill-tempered churl named Chiang Kai-shek served as one of Tu's principal lieutenants.

Born in 1887 on the second floor of a salt store in a small town west of Shanghai, Chiang Kai-shek received a modest education at a school called the Pavilion of Literature, where he studied the book *The Art of War* by Sun Tzu, a fourth-century B.C. teacher who believed "warfare is based on deception." Chiang would wake each day before dawn to meditate for one-half hour. He would visualize himself as the savior of China.

To overcome his loneliness, Chiang married a simple villager, whom he beat frequently when she failed to satisfy his needs.

When Chiang moved to Japan in 1906 to immerse himself in military training, his wife watched him leave with relief. Upon his return to China, Chiang became a hero of the 1911 revolution. After assassinating a rival in a hospital room with a single shot, he escaped to Japan in 1912 to avoid prosecution.

The following year, Chiang returned to China as the chief of security for Dr. Sun and as a leader in the Kuomintang National army. At a Christmas party given by T. V. Soong at Dr. Sun Yat-sen's home, he met the intriguing Mai-ling. Instantly attracted by her charm and political connections, he initiated an all-out assault for her hand. Recognizing Chiang's character shortcomings, Dr. Sun and Ching-ling refused to support his plea for marriage. Nevertheless, Chiang persisted.

In 1925, the 58-year-old Dr. Sun Yat-sen, president extraordinaire of China, died from a liver tumor. Through Chiang's dint of will and strength of arms, the KMT Standing Committee elected him as its chairman. The following May, Chiang Kai-shek became the leader of the party as well.

In an effort to cement his name to that of Dr. Sun, Chiang proposed marriage to the widowed Ching-ling. She declined. Later, Chiang proposed to Mai-ling, who accepted with Ai-ling's encouragement.

Chiang mistrusted the Russians, fearing their potential interference in Chinese affairs. He announced a plan to eliminate all Communists from the KMT. In response, Ching-ling condemned her brother-in-law and called for his dismissal from all posts. Chou En-lai initiated a leftist coup in Shanghai, but the rightist forces maintained control. In disgust, Madame Sun departed China for exile in Russia, where Chiang's government became known as a toilet that as often as you flush it still stinks. Ching-ling would say of her sister that without Mai-ling's soft touch, Chiang "might have been worse."[51]

On December 1, 1927, 30-year-old Mai-ling married Chiang Kai-shek in front of a giant portrait of Dr. Sun. Ai-ling and a host of European, Asian and American dignitaries attended. Ching-ling remained in the chill of a Moscow winter in protest.

Chiang provided Mai-ling with the fame she craved. Mai-ling gave Chiang the pedigree he lacked. However, when Chiang omitted the required bribes to the gangster nicknamed "Bigeared Tu," a car picked up Mai-ling and delivered her to Tu's home, where the Green Gang reminded the newlywed of how dangerous Shanghai could be without protection. The generalissimo and his wife took Tu's message to heart and paid.

At Chiang's urging, TL Soong accompanied his sister Ching-ling from Russia to China for a formal ceremony honoring her dead husband, Dr. Sun. Ching-ling attended but issued a public statement supporting the Communists and repudiating her brother-in-law.

Life in China proved a constant struggle for Mai-ling, nicknamed the "Dragonlady" by her enemies. With the Communists attacking from within and Japan from without, Generalissimo and Madame Chiang felt constant pressure. Yet the public idolized Mai-ling. When Chiang converted to Christianity, the couple became the darlings of the Western press.

The political and social demands of ruling China weighed heavily on Mai-ling. For relaxation, she chain-smoked mentholated English cigarettes in private, which further attacked her health. Madame Chiang also suffered from urticaria, a chronic skin ailment producing angry red splotches whenever she became nervous or excited.

Madame Chiang, aping the "New Deal" of the United States, instituted a "New-Life Movement" for China. Basing her ideas upon the virtues of courtesy, service, honesty and honor, she proposed a series of simple credos such as "good roads" and "love thy neighbor." Although the New-Life Movement proved unpopular in China, foreigners applauded Mai-ling's efforts. She also wrote *Messages in War and Peace,* citing her indignation at the democratic world's refusal to commit adequate aid for her country. She wrote, "Perhaps you can hear over the radio the noise of the cannonade, but hidden from your hearing are the cries of the dying, the pain of the masses of wounded and the tumult of crashing buildings."[52]

Madame Chiang pleaded for help in her "Message to the Women of America" in the *New York Herald Tribune.* "Only by collective action, economic if nothing else, will it be possible to arrest the collapse of democratic ideas. Something must be done immediately to compel Japan to understand that her violation of treaties and her revolting inhumanities can neither be condoned nor excused."[53]

In 1938 *Time* magazine named Generalissimo and Madame Chiang Kai-shek as Man and Woman of the Year to honor their achievements in opposition to the Japanese menace prior to the outbreak of World War II.

Friends reported numerous stories of Mai-ling's bravery. Once she sat on the edge of a bomb shelter as shells exploded in the distance while she edited a draft of a newspaper article seeking military aid. Facing danger on a daily basis, she traveled with her own cook to avoid the risk of being poisoned by her enemies. Madame Chiang's personal vitality provided spirit to her beleaguered country but sapped her strength. Hours of speechmaking, the chilly fog of Chungking, sleepless nights and overwork weakened her body's natural defenses, forcing her to undergo an operation to repair her inflamed sinus.

As Japan attacked China prior to World War II, T. V. Soong hastened to the United States to raise funds for the undercapitalized Chinese army. Madame Chiang accepted responsibility for the air force. She helped to secure the legendary Claire Chennault to whip her Chinese fighter pilots into line. She hired mercenaries to bolster the nationalist forces. United States newspapers featured the comic strip "Terry and the Pirates" patterned upon the Chinese air force. Madame Chiang became the model for the mysterious Dragonlady, who frequently came to the rescue of the fearless American pilots.

By December 1941, the P-40s and "Flying Tigers" had turned the tide. Japanese power in China weakened. Once again, the Communists became Chiang's primary enemies.

As his wife's health declined, the generalissimo sought sex from younger women. Mai-ling fumed at her husband's unfaithfulness.

At Wendell Willkie's suggestion, Madame Chiang visited the United States on a goodwill tour. Time away from her husband provided welcome relief. Rocked by further rumors of her husband's infidelity, Mai-ling struggled to maintain power against Chiang Ching-kuo, her stepson from Chiang's prior marriage. She maneuvered to be her husband's successor if not first in his bedroom.

War and a stressful lifestyle continued to harm Madame Chiang's health. By 1942, exhaustion, a bad back, impacted wisdom teeth, hives and sinus problems aggravated by her chain smoking, combined with an automobile accident, returned her to the hospital. Entering Columbia Presbyterian Medical Center in New York under an assumed name, the 45-year-old celebrity had her wisdom teeth extracted. She spent several weeks recovering at President Roosevelt's Hyde Park retreat following her release from the hospital.

Mai-ling proved a difficult and demanding guest for the Roosevelts. She required her bed to be made up with imported Chinese silk sheets and changed at least once a day, frequently three or four times. Her autocratic political views demonstrated her lack of understanding of the American form of democracy.

Madame Chiang's opulent dress, imperial bearing and expensive jewelry stood in sharp contrast to the poverty of her country, irritating the Roosevelts. When Eleanor asked how she would handle the wartime coal strike in the states, Mai-ling drew her lacquered fingernails across her throat. When Mai-ling finally departed for a West Coast fund-raising tour, President and Mrs. Roosevelt felt like a great weight had been lifted from their lives.

Madame Chiang's external charm enthralled most Americans. Crowds of celebrities welcomed her at receptions to raise money for China. On March 1, 1942, her photograph again graced the cover of *Time* magazine.

Throughout the war years, Mai-ling wrote books about China. *Sian: A Coup D'état, This is Our China* and *China Shall Rise Again* all echoed confidence in her homeland.

In 1943, a healthy Mai-ling returned to Chungking. That same year she took part in the Cairo summit along with her husband, Winston Churchill and Franklin Roosevelt. To his good friend Franklin, Churchill privately belittled the generalissimo by referring to him as "Chiang Cash-My-Check."

Chiang's extramarital dalliances continued to provoke Mai-ling. She mocked her husband in private by claiming he wore his false teeth only for other women. The strain of an unhappy marriage damaged her already fragile health. As the lines on her face hardened, her irritability grew daily. Sister Ai-ling took Mai-ling to Brazil for an extended respite from her husband and her country's problems.

The November 11, 1944, issue of the *London Daily Mail* reported that Madame Chiang had separated from her husband and would establish a home in the United States. Madame refused to return to Chungking and her husband until near war's end.

With the defeat of the Japanese and an end to external aggression, Chiang vowed to crush the Communist opposition. As civil war spread throughout China, the deep-seated unpopularity of Chiang's regime became evident. Although the United States had spent $3 billion in aid supporting the Kuomintang nationalists, of which more than $30 million was pocketed by Chiang's generals, the Communists continued to gain territory and prestige.

The year 1949 spelled the final defeat for the Kuomintang forces on the mainland. In an attempt to gain a peace with honor, the generalissimo resigned his presidency and retired. However, Mao Tse-tung and the Communists refused to accept Chiang's compromise and demanded his unconditional surrender. In response, Chiang Kai-shek fled to Taiwan with nearly 500,000 Nationalist troops, designating Taipei as the country's temporary capital and declaring himself president. While the United States Seventh Fleet patrolled the waters surrounding Taiwan to ward off the threat of potential hostilities, the generalissimo, calling himself an "undiscouraged old soldier," barked threats at the mainland Communists. Madame Chiang wrote *The Sure Victory,* prophesizing an eventual victory over the Communists.

In 1971, Communist China gained admission to the United Nations, and Nationalist China withdrew in protest. As world opinion shifted, Chiang Kai-shek and his wife isolated themselves.

Following her husband's death in 1975 and the succession of her stepson to the presidency, Mai-ling left Taiwan to live in New York. With her political power behind her and weakened by ill health and depression, she lived in seclusion with her two lap dogs and an entourage. She continued to read the *New York Times* every day to keep up with current events.

In 1995, the 97-year-old Madame Chiang attended the 50th anniversary of the end of World War II in Washington, D.C.

Dressed in a stylish black-and-red patterned silk dress with a Mandarin collar, Madame Chiang appeared to be sharp and alert. Still concerned with her personal appearance, she wore her jet black hair in a tight lacquered bun and sported bright red lipstick. Since she had broken a hip, she sat in a special therapeutic chair. However, she spoke proudly about the importance of China in World War II.

At the end of the festivities, Madame Chiang Kai-shek left the room as she had entered it, assisted by her escorts, but proudly and with ceremony. Today, she lives quietly in her New York apartment, contemplating a long life of fame and accomplishment.

Rose Elizabeth Fitzgerald Kennedy (1890–1995)
America's Best Known Mother

John Francis Fitzgerald, barely five feet, seven inches tall, had been a powerful athlete as a youth. Captain of the Boston Latin football team for two years, he entered Harvard Medical School but was forced to quit when his father died unexpectedly. Accepting a job at the Boston Custom House, "Honey Fitz," as he came to be known, ingratiated himself in ward politics. Progressing from the Boston Common Council to the Massachusetts State Senate, Fitz combined a ready smile, a quick tongue and ambition in his soul to become one of the youngest men in the United States House of Representatives and its only Catholic Democrat from New England. Following two terms in Congress, Fitz won election as the mayor of Boston.

In stark contrast to his outgoing personality, John married a taciturn Irishwoman with a fine dark complexion, who provided him with six children. Rose Elizabeth, born on July 22, 1890, came first. Since political commitments often prevented John Fitzgerald from spending time with his family, Rose's mother acted as the head of the household and instructed her children in religion and ethics. During summer vacations when Congress recessed, the family spent time in Maine, where they socialized with other Irish politicians and business leaders including P. J. Kennedy, the father of Rose's future husband and one of the most influential members of the Boston Strategy Board.

Rose's parents took every opportunity to engineer her future success. In order for Rose to marry according to her station, her education, typical for a well-bred lady of that time, centered on manners, reading, language and piano rather than science or math.

In 1908, after her father had been defeated for re-election as mayor and she had graduated from high school, the Fitzgerald family took a two-month grand tour of Europe. At summer's end, Rose entered a convent boarding school in Holland to polish her German and French. Returning home in 1909, 20-year-old Rose completed her formal education with a year at Manhattanville, courses at Boston University and music lessons at the New England Conservatory. She also joined the Ace of Clubs, an organization for women educated abroad, whose members discussed political and historical events. Eventually, Rose would serve as club president.

In 1910, Boston re-elected Fitz as mayor of Boston by the slim plurality of 1,402 votes. That same year Rose debuted before Boston society including the governor of Massachusetts, two congressmen, the entire city council, a bevy of reporters and her beau, Joseph Kennedy. Petite, spirited, attractive and intelligent, this daughter of the powerful Honey Fitz would make an ideal catch.

In 1912, Rose traveled with her father to Baltimore for the Democratic National Convention and the nomination of Woodrow Wilson as the candidate for the presidency of the United States. She also accompanied her father on missions to Panama and Europe as a hostess and interpreter.

Joe Kennedy, a tall, thin, blue-eyed, sandy-haired Irishman, like Rose's father, had graduated from Boston Latin. He had captained the baseball team and served as class president. At Harvard, Joe played football and baseball. A member of the Hasty Pudding Club, he graduated in 1912 and worked as a Massachusetts bank examiner. By the age of 25, and with his father's help, Joseph Kennedy became the youngest bank president in the United States. He and Rose made the perfect couple.

In October 1914, Joseph and Rose married, as had been orchestrated by their fathers. The young couple focused their lives on financial success and power, neither wasting energy on alcohol, tobacco or frivolous living.

Children came quickly to the Kennedy family. Joseph Jr. arrived in 1915, followed by John "Jack," Rosemary, Kathleen, Eunice and Pat. Rose had a maid to help, allowing her plenty of free time.

Following Robert's "Bobby's" birth in 1925, the Kennedy family relocated to New York. After every child, Joe presented Rose with a gift. With her eighth child, Jean, Joe gave her a diamond bracelet. When a friend asked what her husband would give her if she had another child, Joe joked, "A black eye," as he broke into laughter. Edward "Teddy," her ninth and last child, arrived when Rose had reached the age of 41½. All but the last two children had been born at home.

When World War I began, rather than enlist, Joe handed control of the bank to his father in order to become assistant general manager of Bethlehem Steel's Fore River Shipyard in Quincy, Massachusetts. Joe, a diligent worker, developed an ulcer pushing to achieve production figures.

After the armistice, Joe formed a syndicate to purchase a chain of movie theaters, necessitating his departure from home for long periods. According to author Ronald Kessler, Joe Kennedy began an affair with actress Gloria Swanson around this time.

With her husband frequently away, this tiny sparrow of a woman who possessed great inner strength took control of the household. Like her mother before her, Rose single-handedly raised the family. To keep track of the children's statistics, she devised a file card system to catalog birthdates, weights, communions and confirmations. She instituted a variety of structured "learning experiences" for her youngsters, including trips to the cape and moral-building readings.

Rose demanded and received proper behavior from her children. Dinners started on time. Everyone received an opportunity to talk about the day's experiences. She believed children learned to become effective adults while quite young. Rose Kennedy's efforts produced outstanding children.

Joe Jr. played end on the undefeated football team at the prestigious Choate School. He became editor of the yearbook and won the Harvard Football Trophy for scholarship and sportsmanship. Following graduation, he spent a year at the London School of Economics prior to transferring to Harvard, where he played football and rugby, joined the Hasty Pudding Club and graduated cum laude in 1938.

Jack also attended Choate but often was ill. He had a fine sense of humor but pushed the rules to the limit, once pelting friends with the oranges his mother had sent as a gift. His housemaster wrote, "Jack studies at the last minute, keeps appointments late, has little sense of material value and can seldom locate his possessions."[54]

However, Jack possessed a talent for making friends. Although he graduated in the middle of his class, his classmates named Jack the most likely to succeed. Like his older brother, he attended the London School of Economics, but he dropped out after one month due to hepatitis. Transferring to Princeton, Jack left for Arizona to recuperate when the hepatitis flared up again.

While his children completed their education, Joseph developed into a Hollywood movie mogul, merging several studios into RKO. As Joe's career blossomed and the Kennedys grew more prominent, Rose came to the attention of the media, landing on the best-dressed women list.

Joe landed on his feet during the depression, shrewdly selling his stocks prior to the bubble's bursting and becoming one of Franklin Roosevelt's greatest supporters. Although he maneuvered for the secretary of the treasury spot, Roosevelt failed to make an offer. Foreseeing the end to prohibition, Joe Kennedy traveled to Europe to negotiate agreements with leading distilleries, including Haig and Haig and John Dewar and Sons, Ltd.

In 1934, President Roosevelt appointed Joe as the chairman of the Securities and Exchange Commission as a reward for his past political support. In 1936, Joe left the government to help David Sarnoff organize RCA, while writing the book *I'm for Roosevelt*. At year's end, the president named him head of the new Maritime Commission. With Joe preoccupied in Washington, Rose, who loved to travel, took the opportunity to tour Soviet Russia with one of her daughters.

In December 1937, President Roosevelt appointed Joe as the ambassador to the Court of St. James, and the Kennedy clan took London by storm. The ambassador opposed America's entry into the upcoming war and sought to appease the Nazi leadership. As he watched Roosevelt inch the United States toward the Allies, Kennedy disassociated himself from the president, resigning his ambassadorship in November 1940. While Joe faced the ensuing negative publicity, Rose escaped it by traveling to Rio de Janeiro with Eunice.

The Kennedy children continued to move ahead. With his health recovered, Jack transferred to Harvard where he graduated cum laude. His thesis *Why England Slept* became a popular book.

Following the entry of the United States into World War II, Joe Jr. enlisted as a Navy flyer. Jack joined Navy intelligence, transferring to PT Boat 109 in the South Pacific after one year.

Rosemary, mentally and emotionally challenged and frequently difficult to handle, suffered a setback. Joe ordered a lobotomy without consulting his wife. When the operation failed, his daughter required permanent custodial care. This would become the first of many tragedies to befall Rose Kennedy. Although she never forgave her husband for his decision, Rose suffered in silence.

In a fierce naval battle, Lieutenant John Kennedy survived serious wounds during the destruction of his PT boat under enemy fire. While recuperating from related spinal surgery, Jack wrote the book *Profiles in Courage* to help pass the time.

Rose Kennedy suffered a grievous loss when Joe Jr., the family's hope for political prominence, died while on a dangerous mission after his drone exploded. He posthumously received the Navy Cross for bravery. In 1945, the Navy launched the destroyer USS *Joseph P. Kennedy* in his honor, and brother Bobby served on the ship as a seaman.

Less than one month after Joe Jr.'s death, Kathleen's husband, Billy Hartington, a British officer, died on a battlefield in Belgium. Kathleen would die in 1948 when her plane crashed into the side of a mountain in France while she was on vacation, continuing the Kennedy string of bad luck.

In 1946, at war's end, Jack ran for and won his grandfather's old seat in the United States House of Representatives by a 3-to-1 margin. When a politician congratulated John Fitzgerald on Jack's victory with "Someday, who knows, young Jack may be governor," Fitz smiled. "Governor? Someday he'll be president of the United States."[55] In 1948, Jack ran unopposed, and in 1950, he won by a 5-to 1-margin. During that same year, Rose's father died, and Bobby married Ethel.

After consulting his father, Jack decided to make a run for the Senate. Twenty-six-year-old Bobby, a graduate of the University of Virginia Law School, headed Jack's campaign team in the quest for Henry Cabot Lodge's seat. During the campaign, mother Rose gave 33 tea parties for 70,000 guests in support of her son. Rose possessed the dual skills of hobnobbing with the country club set and mingling with the masses. Although Republican Dwight David Eisenhower carried the White House, Democrat Jack took the Senate seat by 70,737 votes.

In 1956, Senator Kennedy delivered the nomination speech for presidential candidate Adlai Stevenson. Jack's boyish appeal overwhelmed the floor. Senator Estes Kefauver beat him for the second spot on the ticket by an eyelash. In 1958, Jack won re-election to the Senate—this time by almost a million votes.

Around this period, the famous Kennedy football games began to gain national attention. As Senator Jack Kennedy, bad back and all, leaped for a pass, Bobby shouted, "Lots of guts, but no sense."[56]

Daughter Eunice had married Sargent Shriver, and Jack married Jackie Bouvier in 1953. Pat married actor Peter Lawford in 1954, and Teddy married Joan Bennett in 1958. To Rose's delight, many grandchildren followed.

In 1960, Jack won the election as the 35th president of the United States against overwhelming odds. Jack Kennedy was a young Catholic with limited party support and no executive experience, running against Richard Nixon, a two-time vice president. Brother Bobby served as his campaign manager.

Rose always regretted not having a photo taken with her son at his inauguration, a double honor for the Kennedys as Jack named Bobby attorney general. Son-in-law Sargent would head the Peace Corps.

Rose frequently substituted for her daughter-in-law Jackie at state functions. While dining with Emperor Haile Selassie of Ethiopia, she discovered their birthdays were one day apart. The two agreed to celebrate them together at a future date.

In December 1961, Joe Kennedy felt faint while golfing. He went home to bed but awoke unable to move the right side of his body. After months of recuperation, Joe struggled until he could stand with the aid of a cane and speak slurred words. That same year, Teddy ran for a Senate seat. Since Teddy wanted to win on his own merits rather than his family name, Jack joked, "My brother is thinking of changing his name from Teddy Kennedy to Teddy Roosevelt."[57]

Teddy defeated George Cabot Lodge, the son of Henry Cabot Lodge Jr., whom Jack previously had beaten, and the great-grandson of Henry Cabot Lodge, who had defeated Rose's father for the Senate in 1916.

Friday, November 22, 1963, delivered a horrible blow to Rose and the United States. An assassin's bullet felled President John F. Kennedy in Dallas. Despite her grief, Rose maintained her faith in God and life, supporting the inauguration of a John F. Kennedy Library in Cambridge, Massachusetts, in her son's honor.

June 1964 brought further family sadness when Teddy nearly died in a plane crash. While forced to spend six months in bed recovering, he wrote *The Fruitful Bough*, a series of anecdotes about his father.

During Teddy's recuperation, Bobby ran for and won a Senate seat in New York by 700,000 votes. In January 1965, two Kennedy brothers answered the roll call in the United States Senate.

Tragedy struck again in 1968. Bobby Kennedy, a Democratic candidate for president, was assassinated during the California presidential primary. Teddy performed the eulogy, describing Bobby as, "a good and decent man, who saw wrong and tried to right it, saw suffering and tried to heal it, saw war and tried to end it."[58]

Rose hid her grief to appear on national television and thanked the public for its prayers, affection and condolences.

In 1969, the Kennedy family suffered the indignity of the "Chappaquiddick Affair," in which a passenger in Teddy's car drowned after he drove his car off a bridge on Martha's Vineyard. Ted had been drinking, and the American public questioned both his judgment and courage.

Joe Kennedy's health deteriorated rapidly after this assault on the family honor, and he died on November 18, 1969. His enemies vilified him as a callously opportunistic, dishonest Nazi sympathizer who had been unfaithful to his marriage vows, but his family idolized him. Rose publicly and privately stood by Joe, overlooking his frailties and admiring his strength.

Rose always maintained a positive outlook in the face of adversity. "God wants us to be happy and take pleasure in life. He doesn't want us to be sad," she philosophized. Since "sedentary people are apt to have sluggish minds," she actively pursued her zest for life.[59]

In the summer of 1970, Rose flew to Switzerland and Greece to visit Jackie and Aristotle Onassis. As she had promised years earlier, Rose continued to Ethiopia and celebrated her birthday with Emperor Haile Selassie, the two conversing in French. In 1972, Rose supported her son-in-law Sargent Shriver's unsuccessful run for the United States vice presidency.

Rose Kennedy received the Tribute to Motherhood Award on her 100th birthday. Her son Edward spoke at the dinner: "In the chaos of our household, she was the quiet at the center of the storm."[60]

Rose Fitzgerald Kennedy's detractors claimed she was remote, obsessed with religion, personal hygiene, travel and designer clothing. Her children felt differently. Rose, a devout Catholic, had a deep inner strength that she attributed to her belief in God. "If God were to take away all His blessings and leave me but one gift, I would ask for faith."[61]

Rose Kennedy left the world a legacy of 30 grandchildren and 41 great-grandchildren. Her daughter Jean was appointed the ambassador to Ireland. Robert Kennedy's son Joseph P. Kennedy II won the House seat vacated by Speaker Tip O'Neill, and his daughter Kathleen Kennedy Townsend became lieutenant governor of Maryland in 1994. Edward's son Patrick Kennedy also won a House seat.

A series of debilitating strokes during her last years confined Rose to a wheelchair, but she retained her optimism to the end. Surrounded by her beloved family, Rose Fitzgerald Kennedy died quietly in her home from complications caused by pneumonia on

January 22, 1995, at the age of 104. Her continued bravery in the face of death and tragedy while never wavering from her belief in the basic goodness of humankind has served as an inspiration to the entire world.

Alfred Mossman Landon (1887–1987)
Governor and Presidential Candidate

Alf Landon, onetime Republican candidate for president of the United States, was born in West Middlesex, Pennsylvania, on September 9, 1887. He grew up in Ohio, attending high school at the Marietta Academy. When his father, an oilman, relocated to Kansas, Alf enrolled as a business major at the University of Kansas, transferring to its law school after one year.

Always popular with his classmates, Alf served as president of the Phi Gamma Delta fraternity, founding his chapter's first newsletter. Although his grades should have disqualified him, the honorary law fraternity elected him to membership when a friend wrote a letter of recommendation summarizing his strengths with the words "He has character and ability. He will make good."[62]

After his graduation, Alf spent three years confined in a bank in Independence, Kansas, before he quit for the freedom and excitement of oil wildcatting.

In 1912, Landon's father attended the Republican National Convention. When Teddy Roosevelt bolted the party following William Taft's nomination as candidate for president, Alf volunteered to organize Montgomery County for Roosevelt and the Bull Moose party, a rather large order for a young man of 25. Although he had difficulty communicating his ideas in a clear and forceful manner, people believed in him and his speaking ability improved throughout the campaign. Woodrow Wilson won the presidency, but Alf Landon made certain Teddy Roosevelt carried the county.

In 1915, Landon married Margaret Fleming, his boyhood sweetheart. The marriage proved brief but happy. Margaret died when their daughter, Margaret Anne, was one year old, shortly before the outbreak of World War I. Following his wife's demise, Alf enlisted in the Chemical Warfare Service and earned a lieutenant's commission.

With the signing of the armistice, Landon left the service to fill in for six weeks as secretary for the governor of Kansas, Henry Allen, a former Teddy Roosevelt booster. He continued his political career as a county committeeman, while growing his oil business into a modest fortune. Recognizing his ability, the Kansas Republican executive committee elected this up-and-coming "square shooter" as its chairman.

In January 1930, Alf married Theo Cobb. The couple produced two children, Nancy and John.

Within two years of the wedding, Landon announced his candidacy for governor of Kansas. An uninspiring speaker, Alf Landon, dressed in oil-field dungarees, high-top boots and a battered brown fedora, drove his car around the state with his daughter Margaret beside him, stumping from whistle stop to whistle stop, wherever voters might listen. He echoed a simple message: "We must stop spending so much money. We must reduce taxes."[63]

The Kansas electorate believed in Landon's message of frugality and elected this unknown Republican lawyer against a massive Democratic national onslaught. Although he never had held an elected office and Franklin Roosevelt carried Kansas by a 74,000 plurality, Alfred Mossman Landon won the statehouse.

Landon kept his promise and set up a "cash basis" balanced budget. To illustrate the seriousness of his resolve, the governor returned $5,000 of his $20,000 salary to the state. During Landon's first year in office, Kansas built an $800,000 surplus.

In 1934, when the Republican delegates met to renominate Alf Landon, one member joked, "Landon robbed both parties of the perennial platform promise to reduce the cost of government."[64] His "horse-sense" approach earned him a second term in the face of a national Democratic Party tidal wave.

The Republicans held scant hope of unseating the popular Democrat president, Franklin D. Roosevelt. However, the party leadership respected Governor Alf Landon's strong executive skills and honesty. Even though Landon declined to enter any presidential primaries and refused to campaign, the delegates at the Republican convention nominated the team of Landon and Frank Knox to oppose Roosevelt and John Garner. Photographs of this midsized sandy-haired, gray-eyed midwesterner with rimless glasses, thinning hair and a broad smile spread across the country's magazines, billboards and newspapers. Landon's book *America at a Crossroads* outlined his philosophy on the economy. He warned the electorate that bookkeeping tricks may be used, but the huge deficit would remain. "The administration has presented no permanent solutions of our major problems. The times demand economy and efficiency so that the regular and extraordinary services of government can be performed without threatening a mighty people with a national bankruptcy."[65]

Governor Landon recognized that his chance for victory was slim. Most of the country had never heard of him, and the electorate refused to accept his dose of pragmatism, overwhelmingly voting to maintain Roosevelt in the White House. The Republican ticket carried only Maine and Vermont. The electoral college voted 523 to 8 against Landon and Knox. Alf Landon accepted his defeat with characteristic dignity, returning to his oil business in Topeka and never seeking public office again. However, the party frequently sought his advice on a variety of political issues.

At the end of World War II, Landon criticized the Morgenthau Plan, which would have destroyed Germany's right to survive, calling it the enemy of God, decency, mercy and common sense. A practical progressive, he supported Harry Truman's Marshall Plan and later Lyndon Johnson's proposal for Medicare.

Alf Landon remained physically active until the final few months of his life. He walked almost a quarter of a mile each day with the aid of his cane and frequently greeted friends along the way. His wife, Theo, often accompanied him.

President Ronald Reagan and Hamilton Fish, who also lived to become a centenarian, traveled to Topeka, Kansas, to pay tribute to Landon on his 100th birthday. Landon modestly described himself as "an oilman who never made a million, a lawyer who never had a case and a politician who carried only Maine and Vermont."[66]

Landon, once of medium build and quite fit, then small and frail, had to be carried back to his bed after about 15 minutes. Alf Landon died on October 12, 1987, just 34 days after his birthday.

Fellow Kansan and Senate Republican leader Robert Dole described Alf Landon as a "legendary Republican who taught generations of politicians what integrity and leadership were all about."[67] Quite fittingly, Alf Landon's daughter, Nancy Landon Kassebaum, followed her father into politics, serving as a United States senator from Kansas.

Lee Meriwether (1862–1966)
Author and Free Thinker

Lee Meriwether was born in Mississippi on Christmas Day 1862, the son of a Confederate officer who had been a civil engineer prior to his tour of service. While away at war, his wife wrote him: "I am pregnant. If it is a boy, let us name him Lee, after the great Virginian, who is driving Yankee armies back North where they belong"[68]— a propitious note in the midst of one of the great tragedies in United States history.

Money came with difficulty to the Meriwether family following the South's defeat. Young Lee found himself forced to drop out of school at the age of 13 in order to help with the family finances, although later he would find time to study law.

In 1885, at the age of 23, after being inspired by reading Edward Gibbon's *The History of the Decline and Fall of the Roman Empire,* Lee paid $25 for a ticket on a tramp steamer to Italy. Tall, slender, dark haired and handsome with a thick but carefully trimmed mustache covering his upper lip and a felt hat tipped to one side setting off his brow, he looked like he might have owned the ship. Lee also visited Turkey and Russia. "I slept in workers' homes, saw what they earned, what they spent and what they ate."[69]

Lee parlayed the overseas acquaintances he made into a series of influential introductions. David Wells, a noted economist, advised him to contact Caroll Wright, United States Commissioner of Labor, who might be willing to pay for his notes about the journey abroad. The commissioner, impressed with the young man's boldness, appointed him as a special agent to gather labor statistics and investigate strikes.

From 1886 to 1889, Meriwether traveled as a government representative throughout the United States for $5 per day plus $4 in expenses. During his spare time Lee wrote two books about his travels: *A Tramp Trip: How to See Europe on 50 Cents a Day* and *The Tramp at Home.*

In 1889, the Missouri miners of Putnam County went on strike. Governor David Francis appointed Meriwether as the Missouri labor commissioner. A state investigator reported that the miners were "anarchists who would rather fight than eat,"[70] and the mine owners called for troops to maintain the peace. To perform his own investigation of the strike, Meriwether "donned shabby clothes and visited the mine, not as an official, but as a man wanting a job."[71] He quickly discovered that the mine owners were paying the workers "not with money, but with checks marked: 'Not good until one year after date.'"[72] Since the miners couldn't afford to wait one year, they were forced to cash their checks at the company stores where prices had been heavily inflated. Shoes that cost $2.50 elsewhere if purchased for money sold for $4.50 in the company store.

Upon uncovering the reason for the unrest, Meriwether returned to Jefferson City and helped write a bill requiring wages to be paid in lawful currency of the United States. A state senator who supported the mine owners threatened to beat "this agitator" to a pulp. However, when Meriwether met the senator in person at a local hotel, he withdrew a pistol from his pocket and pointed it at the bigger man's stomach. The senator turned and fled the room without uttering a word.

Always skillful with words, Meriwether took a position with the National Committee of the Democratic Party to write speeches in support of President Cleveland's re-election.

In 1895, Lee married the lovely Jessie Gair, "whose cheeks were as rosy as the Scotch plaid waist she wore. Her features were fine. Her eyes beamed so that I later called her my beamer."[73]

In 1901, Meriwether ran as an underdog reform candidate for mayor of St. Louis against Boss Ed Butler's machine. Refusing a $50,000 bribe to withdraw, he ran a strong campaign directed against the integrity of his opposition.

The *Republic,* a local newspaper, counterattacked: "Mr Meriwether denounces Boss Butler in public, but in private Meriwether pockets the Boss's money."[74] Meriwether sued the paper for $10,000, representing himself at the trial.

When George Miller, a witness for the *Republic,* reached the stand for questioning, Meriwether asked, "Have you a son?"

"Yes," Miller replied.

"What is his name?" Meriwether continued.

Mr. Miller's face reddened as he answered: "Lee Meriwether Miller."

Meriwether paused momentarily for effect and said, "After hearing me accept Boss Butler's money, you named your baby after me?"

Miller nodded his head, and Meriwether said with a smile, "No man would name his boy after a crook."[75]

The jury believed Meriwether and wanted to award him $25,000 instead of the $10,000 he sought. Although Meriwether won the trial, he lost the closely contested election.

During World War I, Attorney Meriwether served as special assistant to Ambassador William Graves in France. He visited prison camps throughout Corsica and France to ensure tolerable conditions for the German prisoners of war. He resigned his position shortly after Germany's surrender.

Meriwether inherited from his parents both an attraction for controversy and the ability to clearly express his thoughts. Major Meriwether and his wife, as atheists and free thinkers, strongly etched their philosophy into their son's fabric.

Meriwether's mother, a suffragette and editor of a reform paper called the *Tablet,* wrote in her *Recollections of 92 Years:* "In my girlhood I was very religious; the Bible still offers me profit and pleasure, but I do not read it with the reverence I once did. I am no longer able to believe it is God's word."[76]

Later in life, Lee would echo his mother's thoughts:

> The Bible is not God's word. The Bible was written
> by men, many of them savage, crude and ignorant. As
> a consequence I am today an atheist, ostracized by
> some former friends who think an atheist is more evil
> than a man who robs a bank or who rapes and kills a
> 10-year-old girl.
>
> My pamphlets disclosing my doubts have lost me
> many friends, but I am comforted by the belief that
> these pamphlets have helped a little to make people
> think. Therefore, I do not regret publishing them.[77]

Sadly, Meriwether also echoed the deep-seated racism of his
parents. Once, Meriwether's mother complained that a black man
bumped into her and said, "White woman, we's all ekal now. You
gotta get off the sidewalk and let me pass."[78] Mrs. Meriwether,
after spilling some groceries she was carrying into the gutter,
became incensed. That evening she complained to her husband of
the man's effrontery.

A few weeks later, a General Gordon of Georgia, General
Nathan Bedford Forrest and Isham Harris, a former governor of
Tennessee, met at Major Minor Meriwether's house. The purpose
of the meeting was to establish a St. Louis Ku Klux Klan organization to oppose the growing power of the local black population.

Meriwether wrote in his memoirs:

> Some individual Negroes possess high intelligence,
> but history records no instance of a Negro nation pros-
> pering without white help. Under Roman rule Ethiopia
> achieved some civilization, but when Emperor
> Justinian withdrew Rome's legions in the sixth century,
> Ethiopia went to sleep and awoke only in 1930, when
> Italian armies invaded the country and taught it some
> civilization. Until then, Ethiopia had not learned even
> of the wheel.

Only 17 percent of Chicago's population is Negro, but 65 percent of Chicago's crimes are committed by Negroes. Only 19 percent of Detroit's population is Negro, but 80 percent of Detroit's serious crimes are committed by Negroes. Of bastard babies born each year, 20 percent are Negroes; only 2 percent are white. These figures, presented by the Reader's Digest of September, 1962, indicate giving Negroes the right to vote is as tragic an error as it would be to give razors to babies.[79]

When Hudson Strobe, the biographer of Jefferson Davis, asked centenarian Meriwether the secret of his longevity, Meriwether jokingly answered, "To the fact that I never touched tobacco, drank wine, beer or whiskey and fooled around with wild women before I was 14."[80]

Then Meriwether added seriously,

My longevity is due to the fact that my ancestors ate and drank moderately and that Lady Luck favored me.

My mother believed many men dig their own graves with their teeth—that after eating what nourishment requires, they continue to eat merely to please their palate; overeating upsets their stomach and causes dyspepsia and other ills. My mother avoided that ill by baking biscuits as hard and tasteless as rocks. I never ate her biscuits unless I was very hungry.[81]

Actually, luck played a great part in Meriwether's long life. When his cruise ship stopped in Jamaica on the way to New York, Lee and his wife, Jessie, disembarked and decided to remain on the island for a romantic interlude. The cruise ship continued on its journey but sunk off the coast of New York with the loss of all passengers.

World traveler, lawyer, statesman and author, Meriwether provided a study in opposites. Brilliant yet chaotic, bigoted yet openminded, big-hearted but sometimes petty, he suffered more than his share of personal misfortunes, outliving both his children and his two wives. His daughter died in childhood. After he lost his 26-year-old son, Lee Jr., in 1927, he wrote in his memoirs, "He was as vigorous, as virile as the roughest man, but his heart was as tender as the gentlest woman's. Never did he leave the breakfast table but he stopped to print a kiss upon his mother, but he always passed from his mother's chair to mine, and kissed me before he started to his business in the morning."[82]

Following Jessie's death in 1945 after more than 50 years of marriage, Meriwether remarried in 1952 to Ann Rucker, his secretary, who was 37 years his junior. During their wedding dinner, Lee looked adoringly at his new wife and said, "Within three months my clock will have ticked 90 years. It will stop soon and never tick again, but, Ann, I promise my few remaining days will make you happy."[83] Unfortunately, Ann died shortly thereafter following a brief illness.

During the Korean War, Meriwether, a fervent patriot, publicly opposed the United Nations:

> I can understand why Yemen would like a hand in taxing Americans, but I do not understand how any American can favor giving Yemen such a privilege . . . How long shall America continue to let foreign nations which are merely token allies dictate to us how to conduct the Korean War. Let us become so strong that no nation, however much it may envy our wealth, will dare attack us.[84]

In 1963, the State Department announced Lee Meriwether was the first centenarian to be issued a new passport. He promptly returned to Europe to compare it to previous visits. When he reached Madrid with his secretary, a Spanish newspaper noted, "Mr. Lee Meriwether, aged 101 years, is at the Fenix Hotel with his pretty 43-year-old bride. They are spending their honeymoon in Spain."[85]

When other reporters asked if the story was true, Meriwether answered,

No, it isn't true. Blanche is 63 not 43, and she is not my bride; she has been my housekeeper and secretary since 1920. I won't be 101 years old until next December, and I am not spending my honeymoon in Spain. I am here to compare today's Spain with the Spain I saw in 1885 and 1890. Besides, only a lunatic would marry at the age of 101.[86]

An inveterate writer, Meriwether had authored 16 books during his long life, many on travel, including *Afloat and Ashore on the Mediterranean, Seeing Europe by Automobile* and *Europe Now and Then*. In addition, he wrote several books on his life and philosophy, including *My First 98 Years, My First 100 Years* and *Postscript to My Long Life 1862–1964*.

For his 101st birthday, Lee Meriwether enjoyed a hearty breakfast of bacon and eggs, corn bread, orange juice and coffee, then announced he felt "fine." Later in the day he blew out the 101 candles on a cake presented to him at a friend's house.

In March 1964, the 101-year-old Meriwether visited the Kentucky farm where his father had been born in 1827. In April, he drove to Miami and Key West on vacation. Such was Lee Meriwether, a fiercely independent person with an opinion on almost every issue, who persevered throughout his long and full life but who died quietly in St. Louis on March 12, 1966, at the ripe old age of 103. The world lost a peripatetic individualist in Lee Meriwether, whose views often differed from the mainstream, sometimes striking a strident chord, but a man who nonetheless contributed to the richness of free thought.

Sir Moses Montefiore (1784–1885)
Philanthropist

During the time when Joseph and Rachel Montefiore were traveling abroad on business, Moses Montefiore, the eldest of eight brothers and sisters, was born in Livorno, Italy, on July 28, 1784. We know little concerning his childhood and early education, but Moses attended a small private school in Hackney, England, as the son of proper English parents who loved and doted upon their children.

Although the Montefiores struggled to support their large family, they lived a happy life until 1802, when tragedy struck. The 16-year-old sister of Moses died after her dress accidentally caught fire. Friends claimed the despondent father never smiled again. Within two years, Joseph Montefiore died at the age of only 45. Moses, a religious Jew and the oldest surviving male Montefiore, immediately sought and received his father's membership in the Spanish and Portuguese Synagogue.

While still a teenager, the tall, aristocratic-looking Moses Montefiore worked as a clerk for a wholesale tea merchant prior to forming his own stock exchange company. Unfortunately, the business venture failed, and he required nearly a decade to repay his debts, but this young man of impeccable moral character repaid every farthing.

At the age of 25, Moses became a company captain in the Surrey local militia. After the French defeat at Trafalgar and

Napoleon's decline from power, the threat of a French invasion abated, and the militia disbanded.

Freed from the restrictions of the military, Moses set out in search of his future, which included the love of a woman of grace and means. In June 1812, Moses married Judith Cohen, the daughter of a prominent stockbroker and the sister-in-law of the wealthy Nathan Mayer Rothschild. His financial "luck" improved immediately. Although Moses and Judith failed to produce children, the couple gave birth to a lifetime of good deeds.

Years later, on the anniversary of his wedding, Moses, a man who held his emotions in check, would write in his diary, "On this happy day, the 10th of June, 32 years have passed since the almighty God of Israel in His great goodness blessed me with my dear Judith, the cause of my happiness through life. A better and kinder wife never lived."[87]

When his younger brother and partner, Abraham, married Nathan Rothschild's sister, the Rothschild-Montefiore business relationship blossomed, and Moses's wealth multiplied.

Standing six feet, three inches tall, Moses cut an imposing figure. Always well dressed, he selected his words and actions slowly and carefully so as not to offend. With his increased economic stature, he applied for and received a coat of arms etched with the motto "Think and Thank."

In 1824, following the death from consumption of his beloved brother Abraham, the now-wealthy 40-year-old Moses Montefiore retired from the world of buying and selling stocks. Shocked by the savage swiftness of disease and death, he elected to help those less fortunate than he, especially members of his own religion. Since Jews could neither receive college degrees from Oxford or Cambridge nor sit in Parliament, Montefiore felt obligated to improve the opportunities for his own people in England and throughout the world.

In 1827, while visiting the Holy Land, Montefiore purchased a gold ring with the Hebrew inscription *Koneh Hacol*. The words meant "possessor of all things" and referred to a dream he had of Elijah the prophet pointing the way to Jerusalem, the Promised

Land. Moses Montefiore, an inveterate letter writer, noted in his diary, "This day I begin a new era. I fully intend to dedicate much more time to the welfare of the poor and to attend synagogue as regularly as possible."[88]

Moses believed Palestine should belong to the Jews and Jerusalem must become the seat of Jewish power. "By degrees I hope to induce the return of thousands of our brethren to the land of Israel. I am sure they would be happy in the enjoyment of the observance of our holy religion, in a manner which is impossible in Europe," he wrote in his diary.[89]

As he busied himself with county government, charitable affairs and religious life, Montefiore gained recognition. In 1830, the Athenaeum, an organization devoted to the arts and science, whose membership included the Duke of Wellington, John Stuart Mill and Charles Dickens, granted him membership. In 1835, the Board of Deputies of British Jews elected him president. The following year he became a fellow of the Royal Society.

In 1837, Montefiore became sheriff of London and Middlesex. Before accepting the position, he questioned whether it might interfere with his religious and community commitments. In fact, he rescheduled his induction ceremony to avoid a conflict with the Jewish New Year.

Princess Victoria had visited Montefiore's magnificent gardens and estate at East Cliff Lodge prior to her ascension to the throne. In 1838, the new queen knighted Sir Moses Montefiore, whose friends included royalty, aristocrats, scientists, politicians, intellectuals and business leaders. Robert Peel, prime minister of England, wrote to Sir Moses, commending him on his high moral character and encouraging him "to improve the social condition of the Jews in other countries by temperate appeals to the justice and humanity of their rulers."[90]

On February 5, 1840, Father Thomas, the superior of a Capuchin house in Damascus, Syria, disappeared along with his servant. Since witnesses had seen the men in the Jewish quarter of the city, the Jews immediately became suspect. "They planned to use Christian blood to make Passover matzot," spread the accusation of ritual murder.[91]

The French consul to Damascus, the Count of Ratti-Menton, took up the cause against the Jews, and a local Jewish barber and seven of his compatriots found themselves in jail. Sixty Jewish children were confined in a room without food to pressure the prisoners. Although two of the imprisoned Jews, one of whom was more than 80, died under torture and another converted to Islam, all refused to confess.

In March, the Rothschilds received a letter from the Syrian Jewish community begging for help. When the letter was passed on to Sir Moses, he organized a mission to Alexandria, requesting the Egyptians, who occupied Damascus, to intercede on behalf of the Jews.

The Egyptians, swayed by the fervor and eloquence of Sir Moses on behalf of his people, convinced the Syrians to free the Jewish prisoners. The sultan even issued a firman, or edict, guaranteeing the Jews the advantages and privileges accorded to his other subjects. Naturally, the power and prestige of the Montefiore and Rothschild names combined with British, American and Russian support helped the mission to succeed. However, the Capuchin friars refused to forget or forgive the Jews of Damascus for the loss of Father Thomas.

Honors continued to accumulate for Sir Moses, and deservedly so. In 1845, he became the high sheriff of Kent.

In 1846, Sir Moses set out for Russia to protect his people from an edict expelling all Jews from the German-Austrian border. Journeying across rough dirt roads ofttimes blocked by mud or ice, he reached St. Petersburg after nearly one month of rigorous travel. There, Montefiore met with the British foreign minister, requesting his intercession to block the decree.

Count P. D. Kiselev, the chairman of the Russian commission on Jewish matters, unsympathetically stated, "Sir Moses might take the Jews to Palestine or somewhere else."[92] Since his government accused the Jews of being parasites and idlers, he further threatened, "If the Jews fail to master a trade, they will be punished as vagrants."[93]

Although Kiselev eventually promised to present Montefiore's concerns to the czar, the persecution of the Jews continued until Nicholas I died almost a decade later. However, the czar did remove the edict banishing the Jews from his country's borders.

In 1849, Sir Moses set out once more for Damascus to battle renewed charges of ritual murder fueled by the tablet placed in a Capuchin church accusing the Jews of killing Father Thomas. Stopping in France along the way, Montefiore received the support of Emperor Napoleon III to remove the plaque. In Safid and Hebron, Sir Moses distributed sums of money to the needy. While in Nazareth, a woman whose child became lost accused the Jews of killing it. Luckily, the mother discovered her child unharmed, averting a near riot.

Unfortunately, Montefiore's trip to Damascus ended in failure. The friars of the church refused to remove the offending plaque, a grim reminder of anti-Semitism in Syria.

Over the next several years, Sir Moses vigorously pursued his humanitarian commitments. He served as chairman of fine arts on the organization committee for Prince Albert's Great Exhibition of 1851.

In 1855, Sir Moses and Lady Montefiore became the first foreigners to purchase land in Jerusalem, founding a girl's school and an almshouse. Two years later the couple returned to the Holy Land to check on the effectiveness of their donations.

On Rosh Hashanah Eve of September 24, 1862, Moses Montefiore and his wife, who had been bedridden due to ill health, exchanged blessings as they had done for 50 years. A few minutes later, Dr. Thomas Hodgkin, a family friend and traveling companion, entered the dining room and announced the death of Lady Montefiore to her devastated husband. An advocate of female education, Sir Moses founded Judith Lady Montefiore College to honor his wife's memory.

Whenever an anti-Semitic incident arose, Sir Moses would sally forth to the trouble spot. To the question written in chapter 6, verse 8 of Isaiah—"Who shall I send and who will go?"—the answer always seemed to be Moses Montefiore.

In 1863, following the imprisonment of a 15-year-old Jew accused of poisoning his master, Montefiore journeyed to Mogador, Morocco, aboard the British frigate *Magicienne*. While the teenager was being beaten, he implicated a friend, and both boys confessed. Under the pain of the lash, the two prisoners accused others. The Moroccan authorities dragged both boys to the public square, where they were beheaded without benefit of a formal trial.

As the anti-Semitism in Morocco escalated, Sir Moses sought a meeting with Sultan Abul Aziz to discuss the case. Recognizing that Montefiore carried with him the support of England, the sultan, seated on an impressive divan and bedecked in jewels, granted the audience and the promise of protection for his Jewish subjects. Although the remaining Jewish prisoners were given their freedom, Montefiore's visit did little to stem overall discrimination against the Jewish population of Morocco.

For years, the Jews of Romania, conspicuous by their differences in culture, language and dress, had suffered the blame for their country's ills as Christ killers. Huddled into filthy ghettos and denied the benefits of citizenship, the Jews stood as a despised and powerless minority. Anti-Semitic incidents exploded throughout the country, including the attack on a synagogue by a mob armed with hatchets.

On November 13, 1866, the *Jewish Chronicle* wrote, "The most illustrious son of the patriarchs must once more gird up his loins, a man verging upon eighty."[94]

Despite weakening health and advanced years, Montefiore traveled to Romania to meet with Prince Carol to seek his assistance. When an unruly mob gathered outside his rooms at Hotel Ottetelechano threatening his life, the aged aristocrat threw open his window and shouted, "I came here in the name of justice and humanity to plead the cause of innocent sufferers."[95] The old man, displaying a brave and courtly countenance, stilled the crowd, which eventually dispersed.

The mission to Romania proved a success. Moses Montefiore's generous and courageous stance won over Prince Carol, who offered protection to his Jewish subjects.

In 1872, Czar Alexander II invited the 88-year-old Montefiore to Russia to participate in the bicentennial celebration of Peter the Great. Facing the perils of travel at so advanced an age, Sir Moses again pleaded the cause of the Russian Jews.

In 1875, Sir Moses made his seventh and last visit to the Holy Land. He became instrumental in the support and foundation of the Palestine Colonization Fund. However, the weariness of age caused him to resign as president of the Board of Deputies for the English Jews, a position he had held for three decades.

Life had been kind to Moses Montefiore, who remained mentally alert and healthy until his final days. That a man in his 90s would leave the comfort of his home and continue to look after the welfare of his people was remarkable. A savior of the oppressed, a lover of humanity, Sir Moses Montefiore proved to be a gift to his people and all humankind. On his 100th birthday, the Mocatta Library received more than 400 testimonials. Sir Moses died on July 28, 1885, in his 101st year after a long, rewarding and action-filled life. His kindness and charity were remembered by the many hospitals and monuments named in his honor.

Joseph Tilden Montgomery (1876–1984)
A Voice of the Old West

Raconteur, maverick, gambler and political analyst, Joseph Tilden Montgomery was born in Lineville, Iowa, on the Missouri border in August 1876. At age 14, Joe ran away from home, hopping a freight train in search of the excitement of the Wild West. Instead, he learned to sew seed sacks and perform odd farm jobs to eke out a living.

At age 18, he landed in Montana in time to vote for the state capital. A promoter offered him "$10 to vote for the 'right' capital if you're 21."[96] For $10, Joe became 21 and voted for Helena instead of Anaconda as the state capital.

Montgomery drifted from Helena into central Montana's booming gold fields to try prospecting. Along the way he discovered he liked playing cards, a cleaner, more profitable and more exciting occupation than mining.

With the outbreak of the Spanish-American War in 1898, Montgomery enlisted in the army. When Joe learned his unit was scheduled to go to Cuba, he asked for and received a transfer to the Philippines, where he spent two years. On the return trip to the states through the Suez Canal, Joe won $3,000 in a high-stakes card game. "You don't have to be good, just better than whoever you're playing with."[97]

Following his discharge, Joe made a beeline to Montana and the gold fields at Kendall, 15 miles from Lewistown. Since he had a passion for poker, he leased the gambling and bar rights to the Shaules Hotel, also becoming what he called a "pillar of the community." He generally ran the roulette wheel or dealt the faro bank. Although not formally elected, he acted as the mayor and deputy sheriff of the community, chairing meetings and handling minor problems with "horse sense."

Joe loved to gamble. As manager of the Barnes-King Mine baseball team, he hired a pitcher and promised him $150 if he won the game against the Kendall Mine nine. Unfortunately, some "skunks at Kendall" kidnapped his star pitcher and kept him locked up in an old cabin.

When the new minister of the Presbyterian church heard Joe needed a pitcher, he agreed to stand in provided the team attended Sunday services the morning of the game. Joe said, "He gave a pretty good sermon and pitched a pretty good game. The bet was for $1,000, and we decided to give the preacher $250 if we won, but cool as a cucumber, he says, 'Boys, looks like that $1,000 is just the right amount to finish up the church,' so Kendall had a new church."[98]

Joe would bet on anything. He once placed a wager on which log would be the last to fall down the chute at the Jay Gould Mine. Needless to say, he won.

Joe Montgomery knew many of the famous and near-famous. One of his favorites was Calamity Jane, born Martha Jane Canary, from Mercer County, Missouri, where they "raised mules and wild women." A short, stocky lady who wore pants and high-topped boots, she was a bullwhacker (driver) or freighter for the Deadwood stage. When off work, she generally rode a big, old gray horse to the nearest bar looking for a man. Calamity did relish her menfolk.[99]

Joe could spin yarns, some of them tall tales, and he loved people and parties. A short man, barely five feet, seven inches, who never weighed much above 140 pounds, he liked the ladies but never married. He wanted to give all of them an even chance. For a small man, he had a prodigious appetite. He enjoyed eating, especially breakfast, his favorite meal. He also loved to cook. His recipe of baked beans with maple syrup always proved a hit.

Joe became a partner in a small stage line delivering mail and passengers between Kendall, Lewistown, Fort Benton, Great Falls and Harlow over hundreds of miles of rough terrain, actually just prairie tracks, through all kinds of weather. Luckily, robbers never troubled the stage line. However, snowstorms could be worrisome. When a blizzard struck and he lost his sense of direction, Joe would "just slack the lines, and the team would sure remember where the next hay, oats and water was to be found."[100]

Years later, after the gold fields at Kendall had been mined out, Montgomery moved to Lewistown. He worked for the draft board during World War I, registering 10,000 men in a county with only 13,000 residents, mostly men. He also became active in Republican politics, working in numerous campaigns. When his friend Jeanette Rankin ran for Congress, he held an open house in his apartment every Sunday. He would mix up a three-gallon pail of hot-cake batter and fry a batch at nine o'clock in the morning, serving them along with syrup, ham, eggs and beefsteak. He made good coffee, too.

After the war, Joe's Republican cronies had him appointed as the land agent for Lewistown. Thousands of sodbusters returning home from Europe filed for homesteads. In the late '20s when the banks failed, Joe found himself out of a job. When his office closed, he auctioned off his safe for $1.25 to a man who stored "moonshine" in it.

As Joe reached his 90s, Governor John Bonner declared him a Montana state treasure. The governor also made him the host for the 75th anniversary of Custer's Battle of the Little Bighorn for more than 1,200 guests. Joe delivered a speech on Montana before the turn of the century and contrasted those times with the present. In March 1982, the secretary of state honored him as the state's oldest continuous voter.

Joe Montgomery had a knack for telling stories about the Old West. "When you begin to tell tales, you think about truth and legend and a blazing fire to sit beside and a bottle of good bourbon. Truths repeated over a 100-year lifespan become legends. Legends told for 100 years become truth."[101]

Montgomery's flair involved extensive plans for his own funeral. He didn't want it to cost much, specifying a pine-box coffin "like homesteaders used to make to bury their dead."[102] He provided the dimensions: six feet long, two feet in height and two feet wide. He commissioned his nurse to sing three songs: the state song, "Montana," John Denver's "Take Me Home Country Roads" and "America." Joe also directed his friends to have a shot at the Yogo Bar on him.

Although Joe died at the age of 107 at Lewistown's Central Montana Hospital on February 26, 1984, his burial occurred on February 29, Leap Year's Day, just to be different. The undertaker dressed Joe in his favorite bright plaid jacket, red shirt and multi-colored tie.

As state commander of the Spanish-American War veterans and as a colonel in the Montana National Guard, Joe Montgomery received a burial with full military honors. A general and a colonel attended the graveside service to pay tribute along with 16 members of the National Guard.

Just days before he died, Joe still maintained a wonderful outlook: "When I go up to the big pasture in the sky, I go a happy man. It'll be crowded up there with people from the Judith Basin sitting around. They'll say, 'Sit down Joe and have a bourbon with us.' I will, and it will be happy times."[103]

Governor Ted Schwinden sent the following message to the funeral attendees: "Colonel Joe was older than the state of Montana. With his passage we have lost part of our history, but we have retained the heritage of humor and humanity that he left to us as his legacy."[104]

Grandma Moses (1860–1961)
Primitive Folk Artist

Anna Mary Robertson was born on September 7, 1860, the third of 10 children, on a farm in Washington County, New York. Walking in the woods, tapping maple trees for syrup, making tallow candles, taking Saturday afternoon baths in a large tub, and playing games of tag outside her father's flax mill provided Anna with memories of a rustic, happy youth. She remembered her father buying her blank paper and allowing her to draw "lambscapes" of the countryside, which she colored with berries or grape juice.

As Anna approached adolescence, many difficult years followed. At age 12, she left home to work as a hired girl for Mrs. Thomas Whiteside, an older relative who treated her like her own child. This was not an unusual occurrence for a young farm girl of that era. Although Mrs. Whiteside had her cook, wash, iron and do the household chores, she also encouraged Anna Mary, who possessed minimal "book learning," to read the Bible.

In 1886, while working for Mr. and Mrs. Sylvester James as a housekeeper, Anna Mary met her future husband, Thomas Solomon Moses, a farmer. Anna described their relationship as follows: "He found me a good cook, and I found him of good family, very temperate and thrifty."[105]

On September 20, 1887, Anna Mary and Thomas were married on a bright and sunny day. Mary believed that if you were wed on a bright day, a bright life surely would follow.

With only $600 to their name, the couple traveled by train toward North Carolina for employment on a horse farm. Along the way the newlyweds stopped at an inn in Staunton, Virginia, for the night, where friends encouraged them to settle instead of heading farther south.

Buying a cow for $25 and 12 hens for $6, the Moses family set up housekeeping on a rented farm. Anna took the milk from the cows and churned butter, which she sold to a local shopkeeper. Later, she prepared and sold potato chips for profit.

While in Staunton, Anna gave birth to 10 children, half of whom lived: Winona, Lloyd, Anna, Forrest and Hugh.

After almost 20 years of married life in Virginia, Tom became homesick, and the Moses family moved back to a farm in New York, prior to Christmas of 1905.

Farm life meant a fixed routine for Anna: waking at five, making breakfast, milking the cows, doing chores, making lunch, doing more chores, and preparing dinner—possibly reading the Bible—then going to bed at nine, ready for the upcoming sunrise. Yet this simple and busy schedule produced a happy life—that is, until the troubled, blizzard-filled day of January 15, 1927, when Tom returned to the house empty-handed after going outside for wood.

Collapsing into a chair, Tom mumbled, "I'm so cold." Pausing for a breath, he said, "It turned dark all at once."[106] Those were Tom's last words. Adding to Anna's misfortune, daughter Anna caught influenza and died in 1932.

Burying her sadness in hard work and faith in God, Anna Mary continued her busy life on the farm. After all, "idle hands were the devil's handiwork."

Anna Mary always had enjoyed art. Her surviving daughter, Winona, encouraged her to sew worsted pictures for relaxation. As old age and arthritis made sewing increasingly more difficult, she began to paint for relaxation. Postcards depicting far-off places provided her with early models.

After completing several paintings, Anna hung them at the Thomas Drug Store in Hoosick Falls. She also displayed several at the Cambridge Fair along with her canned fruits. She won a prize for the fruits but nothing for the paintings.

When Louis Caldor, an engineer and an art collector, saw the paintings at the drug store, he immediately became attracted to the brightly colored landscapes. Caldor purchased all the paintings on display, paying $3 for the smaller ones and $5 for the larger. Size rather than complexity determined Anna's prices.

Caldor took the paintings to galleries, and three found their way into the Museum of Modern Art. Austrian immigrant and gallery owner Otto Kallir recognized the power in Anna's folk art. Kallir arranged her first one-woman show, "What a Farm Wife Painted," at the Galerie St. Étienne on 57th Street in New York City. When the *New York Herald Tribune* reviewed the exhibit, a desk man included the name "Grandma Moses" in the headline. The name stuck. Large numbers of senior citizens admired the works of Grandma Moses, and the 80-year-old painter became a celebrity.

Asked to appear at Gimbel's Department Store's auditorium, Anna thought she was going to speak to a few friends about her preserves. When someone pinned a microphone on her, the flustered old woman described two jars of preserves she carried in her purse to the audience of 400, who came hoping to obtain an insight into the paintings of Grandma Moses.

When her painting *The Old Oaken Bucket* won first prize at the New York State Fair, critics began to take notice of her feel for rural life.

Anna Mary painted on an old tip-up table, which served as her easel, using masonite or hard wood rather than canvas for durability. Her subjects generally involved simple life on the farm, deceptively primitive but strongly grounded in color and zest. Lacking an understanding of proper proportions and perspective, she concentrated on the romantic realities of farm life such as sugaring-off maple trees, catching a Thanksgiving turkey or cutting down a Christmas tree. A base of luminous white paint added brilliance to many of her paintings.

Using her technique of "first the sky, then the mountains, then the hills, then the trees," Grandma Moses completed more than 1,500 paintings.[107]

"I like pretty things the best. What's the use of painting a picture if it isn't something nice?" Anna Mary explained. She often told her friends in her homespun style, "If I didn't start painting, I would have raised chickens."[108]

In May 1949, the painter received an award from President Truman, who even played the piano for her. The two spent much of their meeting discussing farming techniques.

As the money poured in, Grandma Moses no longer priced her paintings by size. However, she treated her growing wealth naively, sometimes bringing home stacks of cash or forgetting to cash a large check.

Grandma Moses had a wonderful 100th birthday party, but the following summer she suffered a fall from which she never recovered. She slipped away on December 13, 1961, at the age of 101.

"I look back on my life as a good day's work. It was done, and I feel satisfied," this wise old woman wrote during her last days.[109] On her table sat an unfinished painting that she appropriately called *Beautiful World*. The simple strokes of Grandma Moses's brush provided her with the fame she neither sought nor expected but richly deserved.

Scott Nearing (1883–1983)
Author, Educator and Gadfly

Scott Nearing, father of the back-to-the-land movement, believed education should be a lifelong process. He divided humanity into two basic groups: those who followed the path of comfort and those who reveled in the hard life. Nearing opted for the second category.

Raised in a lumber and coal mining camp in the town of Morris Run, Pennsylvania, Scott was the oldest in a family of three brothers and three sisters. The three girls would marry rich men; the three brothers would struggle economically throughout their adult lives.

Scott credited his mother, Minnie Zabriskie Nearing, with encouraging him in his love of nature and books. Although not particularly close to his father, a quiet man who ran the company general store, he adored his grandfather, Winfield Scott Nearing, the superintendent of the town, who taught him science, carpentry and precise thought. Grandpa Nearing was no conformist. When the local minister sought his permission to pray at the Nearing house before a dinner, Winfield replied, "Why not? It won't do no harm."

As a youth, Scott frequented his grandfather's library whenever possible. While working in the company store, the butcher shop and the lumber mill he witnessed the first electric line, flush toilet and telephone in Morris Run.

Scott Nearing, gifted with wonderful genes, had been born into a long-lifed family. As a child he knew all four grandparents, two great-grandfathers and one great-grandmother.

At the age of 13, Scott and the family moved to Philadelphia so the children could attend a public school. However, the Nearings continued to summer at Morris Run.

After graduation from high school, Nearing attended the Wharton School of the University of Pennsylvania ("Penn"), where the highest marks usually accompanied conformity. "The perfect parrot was the perfect pupil."[110]

As a junior at Penn, Nearing wrote a paper enumerating the corruption in Philadelphia ward politics. When during a sermon, a Baptist minister claimed Philadelphia was one of the best-governed cities in the country, Nearing walked out of the church in disgust, never to return.

When Nearing discovered the power of scholastic inspiration during Professor Simon Nelson Patten's Economics 162 class, he chose a career in education, earning dual degrees in oratory and economics in 1905.

The following year, Nearing taught freshman economics at Penn. In addition, he served on the Pennsylvania Child Labor Committee, seeking protective legislation for minors in the workplace. In 1907, the University of Pennsylvania appointed Dr. Nearing as an assistant instructor at $800 per year. In 1908, Nearing co-authored a popular text book, *Economics*. During the same year, he married Nellie Seeds, with whom he had two children.

Between 1911 and 1915, Professor Nearing, a prolific author, wrote six books: *The Solution of the Child Labor Problem, Wages in the United States, Financing the Wage Earner's Family, Reducing the Cost of Living, Riches and Poverty* and *Anthracite*. In 1918, he also found time to co-author *Elements of Economics: With Special Reference to American Conditions,* a book that eventually captured 75 percent of the high school market.

Throughout his writings and lectures, the young professor opposed the power of big business and their abuses of child labor. The dean of the university cautioned him to be less outspoken—

especially since the school depended on public grants and private contributions from wealthy businessmen.

Nearing ignored the warnings, speaking on social issues at Swarthmore, the Philadelphia School for Social Work and Chautauqua. During this time, he shaped and solidified his philosophy of life. He became a full-fledged vegetarian. While studying Leo Tolstoy, the Russian nobleman and author of *War and Peace,* Nearing gained an understanding of the necessity to reduce human suffering, end wars, protect all living beings and act decisively against the world's fires—all within the context of nonviolence.

Nearing's students recognized him as an outstanding teacher and lecturer. However, his radical stance alienated the board of directors of the University of Pennsylvania, who refused to renew his contract in 1916. The academic world overwhelmingly supported Nearing. The *Chicago Herald* commented, "Nearing's unforgivable sin was to talk about wages. He believed that labor ought to be paid enough to support life."[111] The *New York Times* called him the "Philadelphia martyr."[112]

The University of Toledo offered Dr. Nearing a position on its teaching staff as professor of social science but ousted him after one year for his antiwar stance. The federal authorities in Toledo even seized his records as evidence of possible sedition. In 1917, he joined the Socialist Party and taught at the Rand School of Social Science, a leftist institution.

In 1918, Nearing ran for a New York congressional seat on the Socialist ticket against Fiorello LaGuardia. He raged against war in the pamphlet *The Menace of Militarism* and wrote *The Debs Decision* following the trial of Socialist presidential candidate Eugene Debs and his subsequent conviction for an antiwar speech. Dr. Nearing's book *The Great Madness* caused him to be tried for obstructing wartime recruiting efforts under the Espionage Law. Defending himself, Nearing espoused Socialism and his antiwar beliefs. Amazingly, the jury found him not guilty.

With his career in ruins, Nearing grew despondent about capitalism and Western materialism. He believed darkness had taken over the United States. In 1925, he visited Russia to study its school system, writing about his visit in *Education in Soviet*

Russia. During the year, he also authored *Educational Frontiers: Simon Patten and Other Teachers,* a tribute to his friend and former professor.

A trip to China in 1927 led to the book *Whither China?* and Nearing's decision to join the Communist Party. When he chose to publish *The Twilight of Empire* against party opposition, Nearing was forced to resign, although he continued to uphold Communist principles. Thus, Nearing found himself without political ties, alone in a destructive world.

During the '30s, vast impersonal forces swept across the face of history like a tidal wave. After witnessing early Nazi political victories, Nearing wrote *Fascism* to explain dictatorships and planned economies. Numerous visits to Spain, the testing ground for new forces in Europe, provided him with hope that the feudalism of the past might be overturned.

After years of separation from his first wife, Nearing married Helen Knothe, a woman 20 years his junior and a lifelong vegetarian. The couple took up homesteading and organic farming in Vermont.

With the impending approach of World War II, "leftism" had become a dirty word in the United States. Yet in 1943, this citizen of the world helped found "World Events," a leftist newsletter supported by the labor movement. Nearing believed that the United States had squandered its mineral resources on war and poisoned the air, land and water. For almost a decade, the newsletter railed against big business. Nearing believed socialism provided the best avenue to end ignorance, spread knowledge, end poverty and substitute planning for haphazard living. He witnessed the emergence of socialism in many parts of South America, Cuba and Europe with optimism.

Scott and Helen Nearing lived in a peaceful cocoon of tranquility on their farm in Vermont. Nearing wrote about the joy of making maple syrup in his 1950 book, *The Maple Sugar Book.* He described farm life in *Living the Good Life.* Between growing seasons, the Nearings traveled, studied and wrote on a variety of themes.

Scott Nearing attributed his long life to a regimen of physical exercise, abstention from excess and good diet. His meals consisted mostly of fruits and vegetables with enough nuts and protein to provide balance. An organic farmer, he avoided commercial sprays and fertilizers. His lifestyle allowed him to remain physically active until the last few months of his life.

Helen Nearing described her husband's death in the book *Light on Aging and Dying*:

> My husband died with deliberation and in full consciousness. He knew exactly what he was doing and planned it in advance. He was near the end, and he wanted a death by choice—by his own decision. His life had been sane, and he lived quietly and purposively. He wanted to go the same way—to live right into death.
>
> One day, as we were starting our evening meal at the table, he said, "I think I won't eat any more." He was ninety-nine, approaching his hundredth year. His body was wearing out.
>
> From that time—a month before his hundredth birthday—he abstained from all solid food, taking only liquids. He waned and lost his strength, but kept his wits and good cheer. After a month of fasting on vegetable and fruit juice, he announced, "Only water, please."
>
> He had wanted to die at home quietly, and in his own good time—all of which he did.[113]

Scott Nearing died on August 23, 1983, just a few weeks past his 100th birthday.

Dr. Nearing's greatness lay in his willingness to accept the consequences of trying to change the world into a fairer and more humane society. He traded the fame, security and success of the academic world for the knowledge that he had made the effort to do what was right.

Chief William Red Fox (1870–1976)
A Bridge between the Sioux Nation and America's Past

R ed Fox, or To-Ka-Lu-Lu-Ta in his native tongue, was the nephew of the famous war chief Crazy Horse. He was born in a tepee facing the morning sun on June 11, 1870, in the Pine Ridge Reservation at the foothills of the Bighorn Mountains.

One of his earliest memories involved Chief Sitting Bull perched atop a horse. The chief's powerful physique and stern face towered above the six-year-old child prior to the Sioux attack on General Custer at Little Bighorn.

The younger braves despised the ordered life of the reservation. Crazy Horse and his brother-in-law, Black Eagle, who happened to be Red Fox's father, left the reservation for the Big Horn Basin in search of better hunting, although forbidden to do so by treaty. Around the same time, a band of Cheyenne warriors escaped from a reservation in Montana and defeated a troop of soldiers under General George Crook.

In response, General Custer set up camp 20 miles from Red Fox's village. Crazy Horse believed Custer intended to attack and elected to lead an offensive assault. On June 25, 1876, the Sioux forces surrounded the Seventh Cavalry and slaughtered 260 soldiers. Only one soldier, Curley the Crow, survived by playing dead.

Crazy Horse and Sitting Bull fled to Canada. Red Fox and his family returned to the reservation under a heavy army escort. For the balance of his life, Red Fox would mourn that day, that time and the lost spirit of his people.

Eventually, Crazy Horse, recognizing the futility of opposing the white man, returned to his reservation but later departed— without receiving permission from the authorities—to seek help for his ailing wife. Soldiers at the nearby fort tricked him into entering an empty building that contained a cell. When Crazy Horse fought for his freedom, a soldier stuck a bayonet through his back. Crazy Horse's death proved a fatal blow to Sioux independence. Shortly thereafter, Sitting Bull would die from a bullet wound.

The government separated the younger Indians from their parents. Red Fox attended a government boarding school, where he received his English name "William," until he reached the age of 12. After traveling to Kansas City by wagon, where he boarded a train, the first he had ever seen, he found himself transferred to the Carlisle Indian School in central Pennsylvania. The shoes the school issued hurt his feet, and he missed his parents, whom he would not see again until 1889.

Sad and unhappy, he accepted the opportunity to spend his summers aboard a ship as a cabin boy. The sea seemed "like eternity in motion" to Red Fox, who journeyed from Rio de Janeiro and Maine to the West Indies.[114] By the time he was graduated from Carlisle, the youth had learned much about life and the world.

When Red Fox returned home he found his parents living in a small house and dressed in government-issued clothing. After a few days with his family, Red Fox accepted employment as an interpreter with Major James McLaughlin, the agent at the Standing Rock Reservation. Several months later, Red Fox accepted a position in Washington at the Bureau of Indian Affairs in the same capacity.

In 1893, Red Fox returned to Pine Ridge, where Buffalo Bill Cody came to recruit Indians for his Wild West show. The 23-year-old Red Fox signed up as an interpreter in charge of the Indians. Journeying by train to Chicago, he joined the show and toured Oklahoma, Nebraska, Iowa and much of the Midwest.

In Oklahoma, Red Fox visited the great Apache war chief Geronimo, a prisoner at Fort Sill. Geronimo's shoulders sagged, and the fire had faded from his hawklike eyes. He bemoaned the rape of his mother and the murder of his sister. He raged at the dishonor. Although Red Fox pleaded for Geronimo's freedom, the men at the fort refused to release so bitter an enemy.

Red Fox met Thomas Alva Edison, Alexander Graham Bell and the nominee for president of the United States, William McKinley, in Niles, Ohio. Buffalo Bill introduced Red Fox to McKinley prophesying, "You cannot vote, but maybe he will help you get that right by the time of his second term."[115] Red Fox left the meeting with an impression of McKinley's greatness.

In New York, Red Fox met Police Commissioner Theodore Roosevelt after a show. When Buffalo Bill joked that Roosevelt should arrest Red Fox for shooting the stagecoach driver during the act, the commissioner threatened to arrest Buffalo Bill for shooting buffalo. Then Roosevelt smiled at Red Fox after watching him ride and stated, "I thought I knew how to ride a horse, but I am just a conceited amateur."[116]

With the onset of the Spanish-American War, Red Fox enlisted in the navy, where he visited China, Japan and the Philippines. Following his discharge in 1902, he signed on as a second mate on a packet steamer that made the San Francisco-to-Alaska run.

In San Francisco, Red Fox shared a few beers with the writer Jack London, who had been born in 1876, the same year Custer died.

In 1903, Red Fox rejoined the Wild West show at Madison Square Garden. Buffalo Bill greeted him like a prodigal son returning home.

The show featured Will Rogers, "lariat-lingo artist," who was one-eighth Indian. Although the two men became lifelong friends, Will Rogers left Buffalo Bill to become a star in the Broadway production of *Ah, Wilderness.*

In 1905, the Wild West show traveled to England aboard a ship carrying wagons, steers, horses, cowboys and Indians. At one performance, Edward VII, the king of England, played the part of a passenger in a coach, and Red Fox had the distinction of scalping His Highness with a rubber tomahawk.

In Germany, the kaiser came backstage after the show to smoke a peace pipe with Red Fox and the Indians. As the tour continued to Italy, the authorities quarantined the troupe due to the possibility of infectious disease. The horses were confiscated in France. Without animals, the show closed, and Red Fox and his fellow actors boarded a steamship for Philadelphia.

When Buffalo Bill merged his show with Pawnee Bill's, Red Fox left to join the Miller Brothers. Shortly thereafter, he signed a contract with the Inge Company to appear in 10 movies. Additional work with Selig Studio, Warner Brothers and Triangle Productions followed. Usually the parts involved Red Fox killing whites or being killed by them in silent Westerns. However, in *The Round Up,* his name appeared on the billboard.

Between movies, Red Fox lectured on the Chautaqua Circuit, which was owned by evangelist and former ballplayer Billy Sunday and Ruth Bryan, daughter of William Jennings Bryan. He would appear in Indian costume and speak of his early days with the tribe. Although he believed his tongue lacked skill, people thronged to hear him speak.

As Red Fox aged, the sadness of his people weighed heavily on him. Depression tore at his heart. Charles Curtis, a politician of Cherokee descent, introduced Red Fox to the United States Congress, where he begged for fairer treatment of his people. He sought Indian citizenship rights, protection from the wholesale parceling out of reservation lands and reform in the Bureau of Indian Affairs.

The Memoirs of Chief Red Fox, published by McGraw-Hill, led to a major publishing furor in 1972. The 12,000-word section describing the 1890 massacre at Wounded Knee, South Dakota, had been lifted from a history published in 1940. Although McGraw-Hill acknowledged the plagiarism, the company believed events generally occurred as described by Red Fox.

A sought-after guest on television talk shows, Red Fox continued as a spokesman for his people. One of his greatest pleasures in later life was to smoke as many as 18 cigars per day and reminisce about a tumultuous century filled with memories.

William Red Fox died on March 1, 1976, in Corpus Christi, Texas, at the age of 105. His stories provide a wonderful bridge to the history of the Sioux nation and America's past.

George Seldes (1890–1995)
Journalist and Writer

Journalist, author and critic of the press George Seldes grew up without benefit of formal religion as the son of an idealistic, utopian free-thinker father who spoke 11 languages. His mother died when George was six, and he lived in the Hill District of Pittsburgh above his father's drug store. George's idols included thinkers and poets such as Henry David Thoreau and Ralph Waldo Emerson.

Although his older brother, Gilbert, earned a scholarship to Harvard, where he graduated with honors, George, who had been forced to repeat his junior year at Pittsburgh High School, proved an indifferent student and a dropout.

In 1909, Seldes joined the *Pittsburgh Leader* as a cub reporter and jack-of-all-trades at the salary of $3.50 per week. Within a year, the ambitious youth interviewed the fiery William Jennings Bryan, who threw him out for his brash impudence, and Teddy Roosevelt, a plum assignment for so inexperienced a reporter. He even covered financier Andrew Mellon's high-profile divorce.

During meetings with the great and near-great, Seldes often sought out and received free tickets for the theater and symphony. In contrast, his coworkers at the paper fought to attend sporting events.

Seldes interviewed actresses Sarah Bernhardt and Lillian Russell as well as Emma Goldman, the notorious American Communist leader known as "Red Emma," a frequent guest at his father's house. After covering a Reverend Billy Sunday revival meeting and reporting that some "repentant sinners" actually were shills, he promptly lost his job.

The rival *Pittsburgh Post* hired Seldes as a reporter for $24 per week. In 1912, brother Gilbert encouraged him to take a one-year leave of absence to enter Harvard as a "special student." While there, George met future journalists John Reed and Walter Lippmann, the founder of the Harvard Socialist Club.

Returning to Pittsburgh, Seldes lived several months with an aspiring actress who turned out to be a prostitute. When the lovers split, a disenchanted but wiser George left Pittsburgh for the bohemian life of Greenwich Village, while continuing his career in journalism.

Prior to World War I, Seldes interviewed writer Joseph Conrad and his "protégé," Jane Anderson, a "Georgia peach," who one day would broadcast anti-Semitic propaganda for Hitler across the airwaves. Brother Gilbert, already a well-known literary critic, fell madly in love with Jane, but she opted to marry a Spanish nobleman.

With the onset of hostilities, George Seldes joined General John Pershing's army press corps, which included playwrights Damon Runyon and Heywood Broun. He interviewed Lieutenant Colonel Douglas MacArthur and shared a tent with Captain Eddie Rickenbacker, the aviator ace and famous automobile racer. Unfortunately, Rickenbacker later became an automobile executive and professional labor-union buster whose conservatism galled Seldes.

Shortly after Armistice Day, Seldes and three coreporters disobeyed orders and slipped into Germany to interview Field Marshal Paul von Hindenburg, who expressed the opinion that the thousands of fresh American troops spelled the end for his country. The French premier, Georges Clemenceau, demanded a public execution of the reporters, whose actions had violated the armistice and could have jeopardized the peace treaty. Although the lives of the reporters were spared, the "press lords" refused to publish their interview with Hindenburg.

With the end of World War I, Seldes traveled to England and Italy to cover President Wilson's European visit. Around that time he also met Gabriele d'Annunzio, a brilliant poet and author and one of the founding fathers of fascism in Italy. Seldes described D'Annunzio as a dishonorable man who sold the story of his love affair for money, an ungentlemanly and despicable act.

Following a year of travel through Europe, George Seldes took over the Berlin desk for the *Chicago Tribune*. Interviews with physicist Albert Einstein and actor Charlie Chaplin added to the aura of excitement surrounding Berlin in the '20s, a center of sin and rampant inflation.

During the famine of 1922, the journalist visited Russia, photographing politician Leon Trotsky and interviewing Bolshevik leader Vladimir Lenin. Russia expelled Seldes for his failure to clear stories concerning the suffering of the peasant community with the government censors, an embarrassment to that country's leadership.

Upon Seldes's return to the United States, President Calvin Coolidge, anxious for an insight on Russian Communism, questioned him about Lenin and the famine. The newspaperman found the president to be knowledgeable about Soviet affairs. At the president's request, Seldes repeated his comments for Secretary of State Charles Evans Hughes.

Returning to Italy, George Seldes met and socialized with fellow journalist Benito Mussolini, the editor of *Popolo d'Italia,* a small leftist newspaper. In 1924, Mussolini gave Seldes a photograph of himself and a lion cub as a souvenir.

Seldes was a man of high principles who held back nothing in his reporting, regardless of the potential consequences to himself. When he wrote a story accusing his onetime friend, whom he called a "Sawdust Caesar," of orchestrating the murder of a member of the Chamber of Deputies to cover up a bribe, he was forced to flee Italy with Mussolini's dreaded Squadrisi in pursuit.

Seldes frequently visited Dr. Alfred Adler, the father of individual psychology, in Germany between travels. Their discussions provided Seldes with valuable insights into the human psyche. While covering a story in Baghdad, the journalist contracted malaria, becoming a human guinea pig for a new cure, which, luckily, worked.

In 1928, Seldes resigned from the *Chicago Tribune* to write his first book, *You Can't Print That,* a scathing attack on postwar political coverups.

In 1929, 39-year-old George Seldes met 24-year-old Helen Larkin Wiesman, a physics student at the Sorbonne, during a party. The two intellectuals violently disagreed over George's distaste for the Communist dictatorship. However, when the couple again met in 1932, it was "love at second sight." Weeks of nightly dating culminated in a 47-year, quarrel-free marriage.

Fellow writer Sinclair "Red" Lewis loaned the idealistic newlyweds $2,000 to purchase a house built around the time of the Revolutionary War on 125 acres in Vermont. Lewis and Seldes became lifelong friends.

In 1936, Seldes wrote 24 articles for several liberal papers on the Spanish Civil War. He reported the tragedy of Guernica, where Nazi airplanes savagely killed 2,000 citizens of Barcelona. This became the war "that broke the hearts of those preferring good over evil."[117]

The Spanish Civil War brought out the best and the worst in many. Ambassador to the Court of St. James Joseph Kennedy entreated for neutrality in the face of fascism. Actor Errol Flynn, thought by some to be a Nazi spy, used the tragedy of the Spanish Civil War to promote one of his movies.

With the war in Spain ended, Seldes wrote for *Ken,* a magazine "one step left of center," for the princely sum of $150 per week. However, a lack of advertising revenue doomed *Ken* to premature failure.

In 1940, starting with a $3,000 investment, Seldes founded the ultraliberal "In Fact," a newsletter whose circulation grew to 176,000. Contributors included President Harry Truman, Eleanor Roosevelt, columnist Drew Pearson, Vice President Henry Wallace and Secretary of the Interior Harold Ickes. "In Fact," dedicated to honesty and objectivity in journalism, thrived for nearly a decade, largely through the support of a prolabor reading audience.

Editor Seldes railed against the hatemongers of those times: Fulton Lewis Jr., a pro-Hitler newscaster, Westbrook Pegler, a rightist anti-Semite zealot, and George Sokolsky, an anti-unionist of questionable ethics. He interviewed Marshal Tito of Yugoslavia and Vice Premier Matyas Rakosivin of Hungary for "In Fact" along with scores of other famous individuals.

Following World War II, the country's fear of Communism had grown to epic proportions. In 1953, Seldes appeared before Senator Joseph McCarthy's notorious redbaiting Committee on Un-American Activities but was cleared of any "wrongdoing."

Between 1950 and 1979, George and his wife spent 13 winters in his beloved Spain, where he wrote much of *The Great Quotations, Never Tire of Protesting* and *Even the Gods Can't Change History*.

Of all the world's political leaders he ever met, Seldes knew Benito Mussolini the longest. Mussolini once believed they were friends until George penned a series of antifascist articles. In 1924, a spiteful Mussolini pretended the two men never had met. Seldes believed Lenin had the greatest influence on the world's history, whether or not one agreed with his philosophy. Sinclair Lewis remained his favorite friend. Of modern-day muckrakers, Seldes most admired consumer crusader Ralph Nader.

Once Seldes reached 90, the newspapers of the world deluged him for interviews, acknowledging his contributions to journalism. At age 94, after the publication of his book *The Great Thoughts,* the *Los Angeles Times* called him "a living panorama of world history."[118] Longevity proved to be his best revenge against the barons who had controlled the content of the news, whom he had described in his 1935 book *Lords of the Press* and his 1938 book *Freedom of the Press*. He appeared in a cameo role in the movie *Reds* as a witness of the times.

Seldes insisted his trained memory had been his greatest strength as a journalist. He never carried a pencil or paper to an interview. He felt note taking might ruin the dynamics of his interview process. As to why he knew so much, Seldes matter of factly responded in *Witness to a Century,* written during his 97th year, "Because I was there."

George Seldes died at Mount Ascutney Hospital in Windsor, Vermont, on July 2, 1995, at the age of 104.

To paraphrase William White, editor and owner of the *Emporia Gazette*, "The country is safe when the people know the real facts, fairly and honestly presented." Muckraker and iconoclast Seldes uncovered the stories overlooked by others, exposed corruption where he found it and challenged the practices of the country's leading newspapers.

Beatrice Wood (1893–1998)
Mama of Dadaism

Born in San Francisco on March 3, 1893, potter Beatrice Wood displayed a radical spirit even as a young child. The only daughter of wealthy parents, she attended exclusive schools in Paris and New York. At the age of 16, Beatrice talked her mother, the real power around the house, into letting her study painting in France. When her domineering mother visited Beatrice's garret in a small village, she exclaimed, "How can you live in such filth? Look at the cobwebs."[119] Her mother forced her to leave.

Beatrice frequently clashed with her mother, who attempted to mold her daughter in her own image. The young girl's offbeat personality and natural penchant to rebel led to constant friction.

At age 18, Beatrice studied French diction and acting in Paris. With the outbreak of World War I, she returned to New York, where she entered the French Repertory Theater. She played almost 60 roles between 1914 and 1916, but none very well. "I wish I could say I was good," she confessed.[120]

At her mother's behest, Beatrice made her social debut along with the daughter of President Cleveland and her lifelong friend Elizabeth Reynolds. The night bored her, and she fled the cotillion to escape the triviality of the conversation.

Through her friend Elizabeth, the first person to teach Russian at Columbia University, Beatrice met a host of interesting artists including ballet dancers Isadora Duncan and Vaslav Nijinsky, as well as Anna Pavlova's choreographer, who taught her Russian folk dances. Mrs. Wood thought many of her daughter's "artsy" friends were "common."

Although Beatrice was not beautiful in the traditional sense, her dark hair, ready smile and outgoing personality made her attractive to most men. While still in her early 20s, Beatrice Wood experienced her first affair, with 40-year-old French novelist-diplomat Henri-Pierre Roche. Her lover introduced her to his friend Marcel Duchamp, the most celebrated painter of his day. Duchamp liked Beatrice and even printed one of her abstract drawings entitled *Marriage of a Friend* in a small avant-garde magazine he published. The frail aesthetic painter often watched her paint and offered helpful advice while smoking his pipe. During these happy days, Roche instructed Beatrice in the gentle art of love while Duchamp fed her love of art.

Roche and Duchamp copublished *The Blind Man,* a magazine dedicated to Dadaism, a philosophy abandoning the old rules and giving birth to the unfettered philosophy of modern art. Beatrice's name appeared on the masthead as the publisher since both men, who were French citizens living in New York, feared possible reprisals from the "old order." To celebrate the birth of the magazine, a riotous Blindman's Ball was held in Greenwich Village. Beatrice drew an "insolent stick figure thumbing its nose at the world" to advertise the event.[121]

Beatrice ended her relationship with Roche after she discovered he had been unfaithful. To escape her despair, she moved to Montreal to act in the French theater. She moved in with the manager of the theater, a Belgian émigré named Paul with whom she had a non-sexual relationship.

Shocked that her daughter lived with a man out of wedlock, Beatrice's mother threatened suicide. When her father warned, "You are killing your mother," Beatrice responded, "She is killing me. Since I am younger, I should have a chance to live."[122]

To satisfy her parents, Beatrice married this strange man, even though the two were not in love. Beatrice's parents gave the couple $3,000 as a wedding gift.

The marriage proved to be a disaster. Paul never attempted to make love to Beatrice but talked her and her friends out of money to support his "business" in Canada. After spending all his wife's money, Paul pawned her first-edition books to buy some imported candies. After being evicted from their apartment, Beatrice found temporary housing in a small Greenwich Village flat owned by her friend Elizabeth. Paul returned to Canada to look after his "investments." When her friend Marcel Duchamp learned of her neediness, he handed Beatrice $50 in a plain envelope for food.

To earn money, she sold a story to *Woman's Wear Daily* for $10 and acted in vaudeville. Her fellow actors nicknamed her the "Duchess" for her unwillingness to mix with the cast. On a lark, she had a one-night affair with an actor and hated herself for it.

Five months later, Paul returned to extort the $550 she had saved from vaudeville. Beatrice's mother discovered that Paul, an emotionally stilted man, had a wife and child in Belgium. An annulment based upon bigamy ended the marriage, and Beatrice never heard from Paul again.

At age 30, Beatrice fell madly in love with English actor and director Reginald Pole. Always unlucky in love, Beatrice lost Reginald to an 18-year-old.

To pick up the pieces of her shattered shard of a life, Beatrice moved to Hollywood, California, where she joined the Theosophy movement, which followed the tenets of the Indian sage Jiddau Krishnamurti. Shortly after setting up residence, she traveled to Holland as a guest of a girlfriend. Deeply impressed by Holland's "Delft" tiles, upon her return to the states she enrolled in a ceramics class at the Hollywood High School Adult Education Department.

A failure in love, Beatrice Wood sought fulfillment in her art, sublimating her frustration in pottery. She managed to live on $73 per month through the generosity of her friend Elizabeth and gifts from her parents, living a spartan existence while struggling to master her skills. Following her mother's death from cancer, she received $1,000 of railroad bonds, which eased her financial burden.

Around this time Beatrice entered into another odd nonsexual relationship, marrying an older man named Steve Hoag. The couple purchased a small home with a workshop, and Elizabeth backed Beatrice's purchase of a small shop on Sunset Boulevard to sell ceramics. When a flood destroyed the house and workshop, funds from the Red Cross disaster fund put Beatrice back in business.

After a slow start in business, the petite five-foot, three-inch dynamo sold her works through Bullock's, Neiman-Marcus and Gumps department stores, as well as in her own shop. Immersed in art, she felt like a "bride who does not know how to boil eggs. She becomes a good cook by experimentation. That's how I became a potter."[123] Focusing on imagination rather than technique, she developed a variety of luster surfaces using metallic salts to add the effect of diffraction to the appearance of her surfaces. She taught pottery as a sideline at the Happy Valley School in Ojai in an attempt to give back to others what her art had given her.

Tart, ascetic and strong willed, Beatrice refused to accept production work even though she barely earned enough to make ends meet. "Pottery for me is a daily discipline. For creativity to work, the matter side must be strong enough to hold the spirit side. If the form has cracks, the spirit leaks."[124] An admiring friend, the noted author Anais Nin, wrote, "Water poured from one of her jars will taste like wine."[125] Gifted with magic fingers and a whimsical imagination, Beatrice frequently took chances with her art, both in its subject matter and the brilliantly colored glazes that added excitement and vigor to her works.

As her artistic reputation grew, her marriage with Steve soured. Her husband's irritability magnified following a crippling hip operation. She too suffered ill health. A kidney tumor proved benign, but her arthritic neck and vertebrae caused constant pain.

When 80-year-old Steve lost his eyesight, Beatrice institutionalized him in a veterans hospital. The staff refused to put up with his profanity and disruptive behavior, and Beatrice allowed him to return home, where he just sat and awaited his death in 1960.

Freed of the responsibility of caring for Steve, Beatrice exhibited her works in India, visiting Thailand and Japan as well. She would visit India again in 1965 to photograph folk art after receiving an invitation from the Indian Handicraft Board. Along the way she visited Toyko for acupuncture treatments to relieve the pain in her neck.

As Beatrice Wood aged, she traveled with greater frequency. In Peru at the World Art Conference, she met the wife of Israel's Moshe Dayan, who became both a good customer and a close friend. Trips to Ireland for a craft meeting, Italy on pleasure, Israel as a guest of the Dayans and Turkey followed. In Iran, a shipment of vases and glassware became tangled in a mass of customs-clearance red tape. While arguing with the authorities in inclement weather, she developed a horrible case of bronchitis. She thought she was going to die. A dose of medication from a local doctor laced with morphine left her dizzy and confused, causing her to flee the country physically and emotionally spent.

The colorful costumes and sights of Afghanistan proved a delightful surprise to Beatrice, who gradually began to recover in her new surroundings. By the time she reached India, she felt much better. While touring the countryside, she disassociated herself from her own illness and the poverty of the people.

As she aged, Beatrice suffered the losses of her best friends. The passing of Marcel Duchamp, writer Anais Nin, husband Steve and Elizabeth Reynolds Hepgood reminded her that the curse of a long life is seeing so many good people die.

In 1977, Beatrice Wood flew to Paris for the opening of the Pompidou Center's fifth-floor exhibition of Marcel Duchamp's paintings. The museum exhibited the manuscripts of Roche as well. A highlight of the trip included a visit to the 97-year-old artist Gabrielle Picabia.

In 1978, the Philadelphia Museum mounted a retrospective of Beatrice Wood's works. She delivered the keynote lecture entitled "Life with Dada," which opened: "What is Dada about this lecture is that I know nothing about Dada. I was only in love with men connected with it, which I suppose is as near to being Dada as anything."

For her 90th birthday, friends put on a second Blindman's Ball in her honor. Four young men attired in leather carried her into the room on a sequined sedan. Comedienne Lily Tomlin served as the mistress of ceremonies for the evening. That same year Beatrice undertook the new challenge of learning to use a computer.

With her rare and beautiful glazed creations displayed in the Smithsonian and Metropolitan Museums, Beatrice Wood became known as a repository of history as she approached the centenarian mark. Museums, universities and scholars sought out her remembrances on Dadaism. In 1984, California declared this "Dada Mama" as a state treasure, and she was asked to donate her personal papers to the Smithsonian.

In 1987, a 30-minute documentary entitled *Special People— Beatrice Wood* won a gold medal for the best documentary at the International Film and TV Festival held in New York. When producer-director Tom Neff asked her to appear on the *Tonight Show* with Jay Leno, the sassy 98-year-old replied with a wink, "Yes. But I won't sleep with him."[126]

In 1989, the Women's International Center gave Beatrice the Living Legacy Award along with humanitarian Mother Teresa, poet Maya Angelou and actress Greer Garson.

Radical, romantic, irreverent and rebellious, Beatrice Wood led an upside-down life. She never made love to a man she married nor married a man she loved. Hopelessly dreamy even at 100, she habitually dressed in brightly colored saris, her body festooned in chunky sterling silver and turquoise bracelets, earrings and necklace. She hid hearing aids beneath her abundant hairdo. Until her last days, Beatrice Wood lived life as though she were a "32-year-old woman" in her prime.

Beatrice Wood continued to work on clay designs in her home studio through her 103rd year with the help of a servant and a friend, Ram Pravesh Singh. The two managed at least one argument a day. When Beatrice used the term "careful" when she meant "careless," Ram corrected her.

"Well, what of it? I'm a hundred. I can say anything I want. I'm not supposed to speak clearly," she countered.

"Why don't you say what you mean?" Ram demanded.

"But I rarely do. I'm much too smart," the Dada Mama explained.[127]

In 1997, the Whitney Museum displayed Wood's works under the appropriately named title "Making Mischief: Dada Invades New York." The American Craft Museum produced a retrospective entitled "Centennial Tribute to Beatrice Wood."

Beatrice Wood attributed her long life to "chocolate and young men."[128] This lifelong vegetarian who neither drank nor smoked joked: "I wanted to be sober when I was seduced."[129]

Beatrice Wood died in her Ojai home on March 12, 1998, less than two weeks after her 105th birthday. Her friends considered her to be the last living symbol of the art movement known as Dadaism. She left behind a reputation for a zany sense of humor almost as wonderful as her body of museum-quality luster-glazed pottery.

Adolph Zukor (1873–1976)
Visionary Hollywood Producer

Born in Ricse, Hungary, in 1873, Adolph Zukor, while still a baby, lost his father to illness. When his mother died, the seven-year-old boy moved in with a rabbi uncle. At age 12, his uncle apprenticed him to a local retailer. In addition to working a long day, the boy attended night school two evenings a week to improve his reading and writing skills.

As a Jew and an orphan with a limited education, the ambitious youth recognized his limited future in Hungary. Possessing a strong imagination, he wrote the Hungarian Orphan's Bureau in search of money to emigrate to the United States. After obtaining the required permits, the 16-year-old sailed alone to Castle Garden Immigration Center in New York with only $40 sewn inside the lining of his vest. Lacking a plan, Adolph looked up friends of his parents, who provided him with a room and companionship. A few days later his new friends helped him find work at a fur cutter's for $2 per week.

Adolph quickly capitalized on the American woman's love of fur. Opening a manufacturing operation in Chicago, he designed neckpieces from a single animal pelt with the head intact. By his 19th year the young man had accumulated a bank account of $7,000, far more than he might have amassed in a lifetime in Hungary.

In 1897, just a week past his 24th birthday, Adolph married Lottie Kaufman, the niece of a Hungarian business acquaintance. The couple would have two children, Eugene and Mildred.

Shortly after the wedding, Adolph joined forces with Lottie's uncle, Morris Kohn. In 1900, Zukor and his partner relocated their fur business to New York. As a sideline, the furriers invested in a penny arcade on East 14th Street and Broadway. The pair installed 100 peep machines to show moving-picture shorts. Slot machines delivered peanuts and candy, and everything cost just one penny. The basement contained a shooting gallery, punching bags and stationary bicycles—again all for a penny. The enterprise became an instant moneymaker.

In 1903, Zukor expanded to Newark, Philadelphia and Boston. The arcades became so successful that Zukor closed his fur business to work as a concessionaire.

Zukor converted the floor above his New York arcade to a motion picture theater called the Crystal Hall, where audiences could view a 15-minute picture for five cents. Zukor often sat in his theater to watch the movies and judge the reactions of the audience. He built additional theaters in the shape of railroad cars to show travelogues. When the novelty of the new theaters faded, the venture failed.

Undaunted, Zukor interested himself in the production of motion pictures. Pioneering full-length movies for his newly formed Famous Players' Film Company, Zukor produced the 40-minute film *Queen Elizabeth,* starring Sarah Bernhardt, which rented to theaters for the outlandish sum of $50 per day. The five-foot, five-inch, lean-faced, sharp-eyed entrepreneur soon became a giant in the burgeoning film industry when the movie made $200,000. Thomas Edison, the inventor of the Kinetoscope, a peep device, impressed with Zukor's creativity, granted the producer the right to use his technology.

In 1912, Zukor resigned from Loew's Enterprises, the holding company for the nickelodeon houses, to produce classical plays on film as a full-time endeavor.

The Prisoner of Zenda became the first feature motion picture made in the United States. The budget for the film surpassed

$50,000, a colossal sum when one considers that most films cost less than $1,000. Other hits followed including *Tess of the D'Urbervilles* and *The Count of Monte Cristo,* made over three-week periods.

A few months after his 40th birthday, Zukor purchased the entire show and cast of Broadway producer David Belasco's successful show *A Good Little Devil,* which included its star, Mary Pickford. Although the picture performed poorly, Mary Pickford developed into a great screen personality.

As a cost-saving measure, Zukor set up a second studio in Hollywood, an undeveloped suburb of Los Angeles, where some of his greatest struggles involved clashes with his stars. For instance, John Barrymore, a renowned carouser and womanizer, frequently arrived late on the set. Zukor's solution allowed Barrymore to select any starting time between nine and noon—as long as he worked the next eight hours in a row.

In 1915, disaster struck. Zukor's studio in New York burned to the ground. Luckily, the studio's film library had been maintained in a flame-retardant safe. Famous Players survived and thrived.

In 1916, Zukor signed a contract to pay his star Mary Pickford the headline-making sum of $1,040,000 over a two-year period. During that same year Famous Players merged with the Jesse L. Lasky Feature Play Company. Samuel Goldwyn became chairman of the board, Cecil B. De Mille director-general, Jesse Lasky vice president and Adolph Zukor president. When Goldwyn's high-energy approach clashed with Zukor's easygoing style, the two moviemakers parted ways. Goldwyn became the head of rival Metro-Goldwyn-Mayer Studio.

In 1919, Zukor's company purchased 135 theaters in the southern states, guaranteeing his company a film audience. The producer began churning out as many as 60 feature films per year.

Zukor, a believer in the star system, developed a long list of headliners anchored by Mary Pickford, Douglas Fairbanks, William Hart, John Barrymore, George M. Cohan and Fatty Arbuckle. In 1921, actress Virginia Rappe died at a Hollywood party under mysterious circumstances. When the authorities arrested Fatty Arbuckle, a tornado of criticism spewed forth from the public. The negative publicity forced Zukor to shelve several Arbuckle comedies. Even though the authorities dropped formal charges, Arbuckle never again acted in a motion picture.

In 1921, *The Sheik,* starring Rudolph Valentino, set Hollywood on its head. Four years later, Valentino, idolized and mourned by women throughout the country, died from a burst appendix. Zukor served as an honorary pallbearer.

The Covered Wagon in 1924 and Cecil B. De Mille's *The Ten Commandments* the following year became film classics. During the '20s, Gloria Swanson, Pola Negri and the "It Girl," Clara Bow, all on the Zukor payroll, ruled the silver screen.

With his increasing wealth, Zukor began to relax. His son, who had joined the company after serving in World War I, assumed greater responsibility. Zukor purchased a 1,000-acre tract of land in Rockland County, New York. He built an 18-hole golf course and a swimming pool on his "farm." An inveterate card player, Adolph Zukor loved bridge, pinochle and poker, and he usually won.

As radio developed and grew in popularity, Zukor sought new opportunities. His company secured a 50 percent interest in the Columbia Broadcasting System (CBS) further expanding his empire.

Soon, Zukor began releasing films under the Paramount name. After the debut of the talkie *The Jazz Singer,* he secured the Photophone process developed by General Electric and Radio Corporation of America (RCA). The smash hit *Wings,* featuring Gary Cooper, used the new methodology.

Zukor proved atypical of the traditional Hollywood tycoon. Mild-mannered and understated, Adolph combined a businessman's mind with a visionary's dreams. Always looking forward, he gambled with new ideas and techniques, pioneering the motion picture medium as an art form.

Zukor's film contemporaries respected him. When he became excited, he might wave his long and bony hands to make a point, but rarely would he raise his voice in anger.

The late '20s introduced Marlene Dietrich, Gary Cooper, the Marx Brothers and Jeanette MacDonald to the entertainment world. Business seemed to be booming. Paramount's profits in 1930 exceeded $18 million and its assets passed $300 million.

Adolph Zukor and his company had reached the pinnacle of success. However, sales tumbled following the depression. By 1932, Paramount suffered a loss of $21 million. Instead of bailing out, Zukor risked his personal fortune to support the company's market value. When losses continued to mount, creditors forced Paramount into bankruptcy, and Zukor's personal wealth plummeted.

The depression also delivered the death knoll for the flapper age and the birth of the bawdy realism of Mae West. Although in real life Mae neither drank nor smoked, "Come up and see me some time" from the movie *She Done Him Wrong* became as much a part of the '30s as Clara Bow and Rudolph Valentino had been in the '20s.

By 1937, Paramount had climbed out of bankruptcy and hired Frank Freeman to handle Hollywood, providing Chairman Zukor with more free time. Once he had regained his fortune, he spent his days on his farm, while retaining an interest in the company's moneymaking ventures.

Television created vast changes in the entertainment industry. As the new media cut into box office receipts, Zukor initiated various gimmicks to publicize his films. In 1952, Paramount produced Cecil B. De Mille's *The Greatest Show on Earth*, a blockbuster Academy-Award-winning $12 million grosser, a giant profit generator for that time.

As Adolph Zukor aged, the kudos accumulated. In 1953, for his 80th birthday, Bob Hope served as emcee for a banquet in his honor. When Zukor spoke to the crowd of motion picture professionals, he put forward a belief in the importance of technology to the future of Hollywood. He felt 3-D might be one such important advance. He indicated that *Shane*, starring Alan Ladd, which utilized panoramic screen and stereophonic sound, would herald other enhancements in the years ahead.

Zukor maintained a wonderful sense of humor throughout his life. When George Burns asked him how it felt to be 103, Zukor licked his lips, smiled and answered with his thick New York–Hungarian accent, "Georgie, right now I feel as good as I did when I was 102."[130]

Active until the end, Adolph Zukor, a soft-spoken gentleman who had been one of Hollywood's great pioneers, died during his afternoon nap on June 10, 1976, at the age of 103. Many of his motion pictures still reflect a timeless quality and bring the powerful emotions of joy and laughter to the viewing audience.

Part II

<u>100 Centenarians Who Made a Difference</u>

This list of 100 famous and infamous individuals represents a sampling of centenarians whose stories have found their way into newspapers and history books. The author's decision on whom to include certainly is open to discussion. He recognizes that many other centenarians also have made a difference and wishes to salute them all.

Abbot, Dr. Charles Greeley. 101. Astrophysicist and former chief executive officer of the Smithsonian Institution. Received a patent shortly before his 100th birthday for an apparatus to convert the sun's energy to an alternate form of power while creating zero pollution. The Patent Office believed Dr. Abbot to be the oldest inventor ever to receive a patent. Author of *The Earth and the Stars, Great Inventions* and *The Sun and the Welfare of Man.* His research brought him the Draper Gold Medal from the National Academy of Sciences and the Rumford Gold Medal from the American Academy of Arts and Sciences of Boston. Died in Riverdale, Maryland, on December 17, 1973.

Abbott, George. 107. American director and producer of 120 dramas, motion pictures and musicals including *Damn Yankees.* Playwright who cowrote *Three Men on a Horse, Love 'em and Leave 'em* and *Coquette.* Died in Miami, Florida, on January 31, 1995.**

Agostino del Rio, Amelia. 100. Professor and playwright. The prolific writer published more than 45 books of poetry, essays, plays, short stories and art histories, as well as co-authoring *Antologia de la Literatura,* considered to be the Bible of Spanish literature. Head of the Spanish department at Barnard College from 1941 to 1962. Mayor Robert Wagner honored Mrs. Agostino del Rio with a key to the city of New York, and the Institute of Puerto Rico named her the citizen of the year. Died in Spring Lake, New Jersey, on December 11, 1996.

Bain, Dr. Katherine. 101. Pediatrician. Author of the reports leading to childproof safety caps for medicine and safety release standards for refrigerator doors to keep children from being trapped and suffocated. Deputy chief of the Department of Labor's Children's Bureau and assistant to the director of the Public Health Service. Died in Washington, D.C., on January 10, 1999.

Bartlett, Evelyn Fortune. 109. Art collector and patron. Daughter of William Fortune, onetime president of the Indianapolis Telephone Company. Her first marriage was to Eli Lilly, the founder of the giant pharmaceutical company. She later married artist and architect Frederick Bartlett, who helped her to develop into a fine painter in her own right. In 1982, the Smithsonian Institution held a retrospective of her works along with those of her husband. Mrs. Bartlett remained physically active and tended her garden until shortly before her death in Beverly, Massachusetts, on July 1, 1997.

Bassett, Preston R. 100. Aviation pioneer and former president of Sperry Gyroscope Company. Developed high-intensity anti-aircraft searchlight during World War I and later the first automatic pilot. He helped the Air Mail Service establish the first night airfield with beacons and floodlights. Appointed by President Eisenhower to the National Advisory Committee for Aeronautics from 1954 to 1958. Died in Ridgefield, Connecticut, on April 28, 1992.

Berlin, Irving. 101. Writer of 1,500 songs including "God Bless America" and "White Christmas." Died in New York, New York, on September 22, 1989.**

Bernays, Edward. 103. Known as the father of public relations. Author of *Crystallizing Public Opinion*. Nephew of Sigmund Freud. Died in Cambridge, Massachusetts, on March 9, 1995.**

Birnbaum, Aaron. 103. One of the last 20th century "memory painters," who took up the brush at age 70 after his retirement as a clothing manufacturer. Birnbaum romanticized scenes from his youth in Europe, merging them with current New York bridges and houses, all done in vivid colors. A small man, only four feet, nine inches tall, he found fame when the Museum of American Folk Art celebrated his 100th birthday with a huge party in his honor. Died in Brooklyn, New York, on August 7, 1998.

Blake, Eubie. 100. Pianist and composer. Wrote "I'm Just Wild About Harry" among his hits. Died in New York, New York, on February 12, 1983.**

Blumkin, Rose. 104. Russian immigrant who founded the one-million-square-foot Nebraska Furniture Mart, the world's largest furniture store. Nicknamed "Mrs. B," the four-foot, ten-inch dynamo espoused the philosophy of "Sell cheap, tell the truth and don't cheat nobody." She sold her business to Warren Buffett of Berkshire Hathaway in 1984. Although she retired at age 95 in 1989, she opened a rival store called Mrs. B's Clearance and Factory Outlet across the street from the Furniture Mart a few months later. When Buffett purchased the second store in 1992, he readily conceded his previous mistake in failing to ask Mrs. B for a noncompete agreement. Omaha's 76th Street was renamed Mrs. B Street in her honor. Died in Omaha, Nebraska, on August 7, 1998.

Branscomb, Dr. Harvie. 103. Chancellor of Vanderbilt University from 1946 to 1963. Responsible for enhancing the reputation and endowment of one of the South's great academic institutions. First chairman of the United States Advisory Commission for Education Exchange under President Truman. Educational consultant to the World Bank. A former Rhodes scholar who published four books on the cultural roots of Christianity. Served as the dean of Duke University's divinity school after receiving his doctorate at Columbia University. Dr. Branscomb was married for 71 years and left nine great-grandchildren, as well as a brother and two sisters, attesting to the Branscomb family's longevity. Died in Nashville, Tennessee, on July 23, 1998.

Brown, Eleanor McMillen. 100. Interior designer and founder of McMillen Incorporated. Decorated the Blair House and President Lyndon Johnson's private quarters at the White House. Mrs. Brown built a reputation on her ability to combine a great sense of style with a keen sense of business. The French government named her as a Chevalier of the Legion of Honor. Died in New York, New York, on January 30, 1991.

Brown, William Slater. 100. Author of 10 books including *The Burning Wheel,* a novel about the damage caused by wealthy people in a rural area, *World of the Wind* and *Ethan Allen and the Green Mountain Boys.* Brown spent the first half of his life drinking, smoking and womanizing before discovering religion. As a pacifist, he served in the Ambulance Corps during World War I. The French imprisoned Brown and poet E E Cummings for publishing unflattering letters describing a rebellion among the country's troops that the army was attempting to conceal. A great raconteur, he loved to tell stories about his life and the lives of others. Died in Rockport, Massachusetts, on June 28, 1997.

Burns, George. 100. Actor and comedian. Died in Beverly Hills, California, on March 9, 1996.**

Caesar, Irving. 101. Lyricist of more than 1,000 songs including "Tea for Two," "Swanee" and "Is It True What They Say about Dixie?" Charter member of the American Society of Composers, Authors and Publishers. "Sometimes I write lousy, but always fast," he joked about his simple direct lyrics.[131] Died in New York, New York, on December 18, 1996.

Calment, Jeanne. 122. Authenticated as the world's oldest human. She had flirted with Vincent van Gogh as a teenager. "I was very pretty, but all he wanted to discuss was painting. People called him 'fada,' touched by the faeries," she fumed, still annoyed at the painter's slight. At age 117 when an interviewer took his leave by telling her, "Until next year, perhaps," she answered, "I don't see why not. You don't look so bad to me."[132] She released a CD at age 121 entitled *Time's Mistress.* She ate more than two pounds of chocolate a week and claimed the key to her long life was port wine and olive oil. Mrs. Calment smoked until she was 120 and was in reasonably good health up to that time, although almost blind and deaf. Died in Arles, France, on August 4, 1997.

Carder, Frederick. 100. Founder of Steuben Glass. Died in Corning, New York, on December 10, 1963.**

Carret, Philip Lord. 101. Founder of the Pioneer Fund, one of the country's first mutual funds. Lifelong friend and co-investor with Warren Buffett of Berkshire Hathaway, who stated, "Philip Carrett has the best long-term investment record of anyone I know."[133] Author of *Buying a Bond* and *The Art of Speculation*. Proponent of the "value" school of investing. As one of Harvard's oldest living graduates, he led its alumni parade in 1997. Died in Mount Vernon, New York, on May 28, 1998.

Clark, Amasa Gleason. 102. Veteran of the Mexican War of 1846. Farmer and pioneer of the Old West. Died in San Antonio, Texas, on January 28, 1927.**

Colcord, R. K. 100. Republican governor of Nevada, 1890–1894. Superintendent of the Carson City Mint. Smoked cigars until late in life and bragged that he lived 20 years longer than he deserved. Died in Carson City, Nevada, on October 30, 1939.

Coolidge, Dr. William D. 101. Developer of the modern x-ray tube and the ductile tungsten filament used in the electric light bulb. Former director of research for General Electric and holder of 83 separate patents. Member of the National Inventors Hall of Fame. For his 101st birthday, Dr. Herman Liebhafsky presented him with a 100-page biography, *William David Coolidge: A Centenarian and His Work*. Died in Schenectady, New York, on February 3, 1975.

Cosel, Miriam Marlin. 101. Former first lady of New Castle and early prohibitionist, pacifist, American Red Cross activist and proponent for the rights of women. Played basketball in high school with the future wife of actor Spencer Tracy. Attended Viscount Peace Conference in 1931. Organized a Canteen Corps shortly after the onset of World War II. Chairwoman of the Pennsylvania Federation of Women's Clubs. A woman of silent dignity who always saw the good in every person or situation. Died in New Castle, Pennsylvania, on December 16, 1996. Brother Ted Marlin, a fine athlete who was born in 1897 and later won 11 letters in high school, died at the age of 100 in Tucson, Arizona, on June 18, 1997.

Crooks, Hulda. 101. Ardent mountain climber and the oldest person to scale 14,459-foot Mount Whitney at age 91. A peak was named in her honor. Author of *Conquering Life's Mountains.* Died in Loma Linda, California, on November 23, 1997.

Dearmer, Geoffrey. 103. Poet known for the *Sentinel,* describing the English defeat at Gallipoli. Onetime BBC executive who wrote wartime poetry with a dignity approaching grandeur. Died at Birchington-on-Sea, England, on August 21, 1996.

Delany, Bessie. 104. Co-author with her sister of *Having Our Say* and one of the first African American female dentists in the United States. Died in Mt. Vernon, New York, on September 26, 1995. Bessie's sister Sadie Delany, a teacher, wrote *On My Own at 107: Reflections on Life without Bessie.* Both women believed in a simple life, good food and no "husband to worry you to death." Sadie, who was born in 1889, died in Mt. Vernon, New York, on January 25, 1999, at the age of 109.**

Douglas, Marjory Stoneman. 108. Spirited writer and environmentalist known as the "Patron Saint of the Everglades." Author of *The Everglades: River of Grass.* Wrote numerous short stories and novels including *Road to the Sun, The Key to Paris* and her autobiography, *Voice of the River.* Died in Miami, Florida, on May 14, 1998.**

Dulles, Eleanor Lansing. 101. German-economic specialist for the State Department. Sister of Secretary of State John Foster Dulles and CIA head Allan Welsh Dulles. Author of 12 books including her memoirs, *Eleanor Lansing Dulles: Chances of a Lifetime.* Died in Washington, D.C., on October 30, 1996.**

Eliot, Dr. Abigail Adams. 100. Harvard-educated social worker whose life revolved around the children of the world. Cofounder of the Ruggles Street Nursery School in Boston, Massachusetts. Secretary-treasurer of the National Association for Nursery

Education. Member of the Roosevelt administration's National Advisory Committee for Federal Emergency Relief for Needy Children. Died in Concord, Massachusetts, on October 29, 1992.

Eyre de Lanux, Elizabeth. 102. Designer, writer and illustrator specializing in 1920s Art Deco furnishings. Created lacquered furniture and geometric-patterned rugs produced in Paris. Friends with literary and art giants including Hemingway, Picasso, Gide and Matisse. In later life, she illustrated children's books such as *Overheard in a Bubble Chamber* by Lillian Morrison. Died in New York, New York, on September 8, 1996.

Ffrangcon-Davies, Gwen. 101. Classical Shakespearean actress whose career spanned eight decades. Critics acclaimed her as the finest Juliet of her age in 1924, when she played opposite John Gielgud's Romeo. Died in London, England, on January 27, 1992.

Fish, Hamilton. 102. United States representative from New York from 1921 to 1945. Opposed the country's entry into World War II. Died in Cold Spring, New York, on January 18, 1991.**

Flye, Reverend James H. 100. This kindly and modest Yale-educated Episcopal priest and teacher's 30 years of correspondence with his star pupil, Pulitzer Prize–winning writer James Agee, resulted in two separate books. His photographs, mostly of children from Harlem and Greenwich Village during the '30s, were grouped together and exhibited under the title of "Through the Eyes of a Teacher." Died in Sewanee, Tennessee, on April 12, 1985.

Frooks, Dorothy. 100. Lawyer and author of half a dozen books. Received a gold medal from President Woodrow Wilson for her help in recruiting 30,000 men into the navy during World War I. Served as an army judge advocate during World War II. She conceived the idea of a small claims court and lobbied until the first was signed into law by her old friend and former suitor, Mayor Fiorello La Guardia. Founder of the *Murray Hill News*. Died in New York, New York, on April 13, 1997.

Gans, Dr. Roma. 102. Professor of education at Teachers College of Columbia University. Inspired children with the joys of reading through books such as *Let's Read* and *Find Out*. Author of *Guiding Children's Reading through Experience, Common Sense in Teaching Reading* and *When Birds Change Their Feathers*. Past chairman of the Citizen's Committee for the Children of New York City, an organization active in child welfare work. Died in Pittsfield, Massachusetts, on October 4, 1996.

Gaylord, Edward King. 101. Publisher of the *Daily Oklahoman,* a morning newspaper, and the *Oklahoma City Times,* the city's evening paper. Also owned five television stations and one radio station. Served as a former director for the Associated Press. Died in Oklahoma City, Oklahoma, on May 31, 1974.

Goetz, Delia. 100. Author of scores of children's adventure and travel books including *The Dragon and the Eagle, Neighbors to the South* and *Panchita, A Little Girl of Guatamala*. Died in Washington, D.C., on June 26, 1996.

Goldfrank, Esther Schiff. 100. Author of numerous monographs on the Pueblo Indians including "The Social and Ceremonial Organization of Conchiti." Onetime assistant to the renowned German cultural anthropologist Franz Boas. Privately published her memoirs, *Notes on an Undirected Life*. Died in Mamaroneck, New York, on April 23, 1997.

Goodman, Milton. 102. President of the Lawrence C. Gumbinner Advertising Agency and creator of the 1950s "It leaves you breathless" campaign for Smirnoff Vodka. Died in New York, New York, on October 5, 1996.

Gosnell, Dr. Harold Foote. 100. Political science professor from the University of Chicago who concentrated on the study of voter behavior. Onetime operations officer for the Department of State who authored numerous books including *Champion Campaigner: Franklin D. Roosevelt, Negro Politicians in Chicago* and *Boss*

Platt and His New York Machine. Died in Bethesda, Maryland, on January 8, 1997.

Granville, Lord Edgar. 100. Oldest active member of the British Parliament. Wounded at the Battle of Gallipoli in Turkey during World War I in 1915. Recovered to take part in the victory at Beersheba, but eventually was sent back to Cairo due to complications from his wounds, dysentery and jaundice. Entered the House of Commons in 1929. Named Baron Granville of Eye in 1967 by Prime Minister Harold Wilson. Authored two novels: *The Domino* and *The Peking Pigeon.* Died in London, England, on February 14, 1998, two days after making an appearance at the House of Lords to celebrate his 100th birthday.

Griffith, Dr. Ernest Stacey. 100. Onetime director of the United States Congressional Research Group and the Legislative Reference Service of the Library of Congress. A former Rhodes scholar who served on the faculty of prestigious universities such as Harvard, Princeton, and Washington University. First dean of American University's School of International Service and the Syracuse University School of Graduate Studies. Author of *The American System of Government.* Treasurer of the Wilderness Society from 1942 to 1972. Died in Portland, Oregon, on January 17, 1997.

Hamburger, Rose Rosenbaum. 105. Racing handicapper who wrote for the *New York Post* under the nickname "Gamblin Rose." She became the first woman licensed to sell real estate in Baltimore, Maryland. Retired as rental agent in Manhattan at the age of 100 to concentrate on racing. Her last selection came home a winner at Saratoga 10 days before she died in New York, New York, on August 6, 1996.

Hargens, Charles W. 103. Western artist who sketched book covers for Zane Grey. His art also appeared in magazines such as the *Saturday Evening Post, Collier's, McCall's* and *Boys' Life.* Died in Doylestown, Pennsylvania, on January 30, 1997.

Hartshorne, Dr. Charles. One of the 20th century's foremost philosophers of theology. Born on June 5, 1897, in Kittanning, Pennsylvania, the son of an Episcopal minister. "Without God, how can we know what is true?" he posed.[134] Author of more than 20 books including *Insights and Oversights of Great Thinkers: An Evaluation of Western Philosophy, Omnipotence and Other Theological Mistakes, A Natural Theology of our Time* and his autobiography, *The Darkness and the Light: A Philosopher Reflects upon His Fortunate Career and Those Who Made It Possible.* Past president of the Western Division of the American Philosophical Association, the Society for Philosophy of Religion and the Metaphysical Society of America. He also is an expert ornithologist authoring *Born to Sing,* a book theorizing that certain varieties of birds have evolved an appreciation of melody. A life-long vegetarian who never learned to drive a car, he bicycled everywhere until a few years ago. Reflecting philosophically on his 100th birthday, he mused that we live in a century in which everything has already been said and the challenge is to know which statements to deny.

Heiskell, John N. 100. Editor of the *Arkansas Gazette* for 70 years and the oldest newspaper editor in the United States. Worked at the newsroom until age 99, but still dictated editorial comments over the phone after his 100th birthday. His newspaper opposed Governor Orville Faubus during the 1957 desegregation controversy at Central High School, a move that cost his paper a $2 million loss in circulation and advertising revenues. However, the paper received a Pulitzer gold medal for meritorious public service the following year. Mr. Heiskell believed in being "loud as it pleases in its editorial columns, but absolutely factual in its news columns."[135] Died in Little Rock, Arkansas, on December 28, 1972.

Hodges, Dr. Paul Chesley. 103. Founding chairman of the radiology department at the University of Chicago Medical Center and inventor of numerous diagnostic devices. A habitual tinkerer, he devised a photo timer in 1942 that automatically calculated the optimal x-ray exposure. Published scores of articles on clinical radiology and several books including the biography *The Life and*

Times of Emil Grubbe. Died in Green Bay, Wisconsin, on December 27, 1996.

Hoff, Chester Cornelius. 107. New York Highlander major league baseball pitcher from 1911 to 1915. Although he had only a 2-and-4 record, the 20-year-old left-hander struck out the incomparable Ty Cobb during his second appearance. After Cobb fouled off two fastballs, "the third strike I give him the fast curve. I throwed a perfect strike over there, and he just looked at it. It was the biggest thrill I ever had."[136] He joked with the Yankees, who honored him on his 100th birthday, "I think I could still pitch nine innings. I might give it a try considering the salaries they're making now."[137] Died in Daytona Beach, Florida, on September 17, 1998.

Horween, Ralph. 100. Patent attorney and first 100-year-old former professional football player. Fullback on Harvard team that won the 1920 Rose Bowl. Played with the Chicago Cardinals from 1921 to 1923, teaming up with his brother Arnold. Returned to Harvard for his law degree. Later served on a federal board administering oil permits. Died in Charlottesville, Virginia, on May 26, 1997.

Horwitz, Jacob H. 100. Fashion innovator who helped create the "Junior Miss" line of clothing for teenage girls. Winner of the Coty Award in 1946 and the American Fashion Critics Award in 1947. One of the founders of the Long Island Jewish Medical Center in New Hyde Park, Long Island. Helped create the Costume Institute at the Metropolitan Museum of Art. Fought with the United States Cavalry under General John Pershing against Pancho Villa along the Mexican border and in World War I in France. Died in Lawrence, New York, on October 8, 1992.

Hsiang-Pai, Ma. 100. Secretary of foreign affairs for the Manchu dynasty. Latin scholar who founded Aurora University and later Fuhtan College, where he served as its president. Author of many books including *The History of Spiritualism*. Died in Lingshan, China, on November 4, 1939.

Jackson, Admiral Richard Harrison. 105. Commander in chief of the Navy Battle Fleet. Graduated near the bottom of his class at Annapolis in 1887. Served aboard the torpedo boat *Foote* during the Spanish-American War, where he distinguished himself for gallantry. Representative for the United States Navy at Paris during World War I. Retired with four stars. Died in San Diego, California, on October 2, 1971.

Johnson, Albin. 102. Diplomat and foreign correspondent. Reported the rise of Hitler and Mussolini. Described the Nazi destruction of the Warsaw ghetto in June 1943 for the North American Newspaper Alliance. During World War II, Johnson also undertook secret intelligence-gathering missions. He became a member of the American delegation to the United Nations Atomic Energy Commission from 1946 to 1950 and the first secretary and public relations officer of the Swedish Embassy from 1951 to 1952. Died in Osterville, Mississippi, on November 17, 1992.

Junger, Ernst. 102. Warrior-author of more than 50 books. Wounded seven times during World War I. Earned the Knights Cross of the House of Hohenzollern and the Pour le Merite, Germany's highest medal for bravery. Authored *Stahlgewitten* (Storm of Steel: From the Diary of a German Storm-Troop Officer of the Western Front) followed by *Storm and Fire and Blood*. Death and heroism fascinated Junger, figuring prominently in most of his novels. When Hitler incorporated Junger's literature into party prejudices, some critics labeled the writer as a Nazi apologist. Junger neither joined nor supported the Nazis and wrote, "The more the panic grows, the more uplifting the image of a man who refuses to bow to the terror."[138] He also described his excursions into the drugs LSD and mescaline in *Approaches, Drugs and the Buzz*. Awarded the Goethe Prize by the city of Frankfurt. Died in Wilflinger, Germany, on February 17, 1998.

Kai-shek, Mai-ling Soong (Madame Chiang). Born on February 12, 1897. Widow of the Kuomintang leader of Taiwan. Celebrated 100th birthday in New York City on February 12, 1997.**

Kaplan, Lazare. 102. Cutter of the 726-carat Jonker Diamond. Founder of the first publicly traded diamond company in the United States, today well known for its "ideal cuts." First person elected to the Diamond Hall of Fame in 1979. Died in Lew Beach, New York, on February 12, 1986.

Kennedy, Rose Fitzgerald. 104. Mother of President John Kennedy, Attorney General Robert Kennedy, Senator Edward Kennedy. Wife of Ambassador to the Court of St. James Joseph Kennedy and daughter of a member of the House of Representatives. Died in Hyannis Port, Massachusetts, on January 22, 1995.**

Kitchell, Alma. 103. Contralto known as the "Golden Voice of the Golden Age of Radio." Sang a solo in the first televised opera. Presided over television's first cooking show. Popularized the wartime slogan "A Stamp a Day for the Man Who's Away" to help sell bonds. Hosted numerous women's shows including *Let's Talk It Over* and *Women's Exchange,* responding to telephone calls or interviewing prominent women such as Eleanor Roosevelt. Died in Sarasota, Florida, on November 13, 1996.

Kleinschmidt, Edward E. 101. Invented the teletype machine in 1914. Held 119 patents as diverse as the high-speed ticker tape used in the stock market and the automatic fishing reel. Founded Teletype Corporation, which was merged into American Telephone and Telegraph in 1930. Awarded the prestigious John Price Wetherill Medal from the Franklin Institue of Philadelphia in 1940. He was still "tinkering" at age 94 when he received a patent for a miniature teletype. Died in Canaan, Connecticut, on August 9, 1977.

Landon, Alf. 100. Governor of Kansas and Republican candidate for president of the United States in 1936. Died in Topeka, Kansas, on October 12, 1987.**

Lape, Esther. 100. Social scientist who led the unsuccessful battle in the '20s and '30s for United States' participation in the World Court. President Calvin Coolidge sent Miss Lape to Europe on a fact-finding mission for the proposed Permanent Court of International Justice, which United States never joined. Played a role in winning United States' recognition of the Soviet Union in 1933. Director of the American Foundation for Studies in Government for 30 years. Close friend and confidant of Eleanor Roosevelt. Wrote numerous articles on women's rights and problems faced by immigrants. Author of *American Medicine: Expert Testimony Out of Court*. Died in New York, New York, on May 17, 1981.

Lowe, Adolph. 102. German-born economist and author of *On Economic Knowledge, The Path of Economic Growth, The Price of Liberty* and his final book, *Has Freedom a Future?*, which calls for a revitalization of the Western tradition of "individualism rooted in social responsibility." Focused upon technological change as a prime cause of the destabilization of industrial economics. Jewish intellectual and adviser to the Weimar government. Professor at Goethe University who was fired by the Hitler regime and fled to England to teach at the University of Manchester before accepting an offer at the New School for Social Research in New York. Died in Wolfenbuttel, Germany, on June 3, 1995.

Mahle, Louis W. 101. Inventor of Chiclets chewing gum, which he named for the chicle tree. Director of product research for the Frank H. Fleer Corporation. Charter member of the Institute of Food Technologists. Wrote articles about chewing gum for *Encyclopedia Brittanica* and appeared on the television program *What's My Line?* He stumped the panel as they could not imagine such a distinguished-looking gentleman in the chewing-gum business. Died in Ambler, Pennsylvania, on February 13, 1998.

Meilleur, Marie Louise Levesque Chasse. 117. At one time the oldest authenticated living person in the world. Mother of 10 children with 85 grandchildren, 80 great-grandchildren, 57 great-great-grandchildren and 4 great-great-great-grandchildren. Attributed her longevity to hard work. Quit smoking at age 90, but still occasionally drank a glass of wine. Died in a nursing home in North Bay, Ontario, Canada, on April 14, 1998.

Meriwether, Lee. 103. Lawyer, politician and author of *Postscript to My Long Life*. Died in St. Louis, Missouri, on March 12, 1966.**

Mills, Victor. 100. Proctor and Gamble chemical engineer who led the team that developed Pampers disposable diapers. He also had a hand in improving or creating diverse products ranging from Pringles potato chips to Ivory soap. During World War II, he helped refine the process for making synthetic rubber. Died in Tucson, Arizona, on November 1, 1997.

Mitchison, Lady Naomi Margaret Haldane. 101. Author of more than 70 books on ancient Greece, socialism, science fiction, fascism in Spain, African independence and home rule for Scotland. Wrote her own memoirs in 1985 entitled *Among You Taking Notes*. Free thinker and believer in free love, bohemian, feminist and commanding presence. Championed birth control in the '30s and rebeled against social restrictions. Once threw a half-stuffed partridge at a Labor Party leader with whom she disagreed on an issue. When asked on her 90th birthday if she had any regrets, she smiled and answered, "Yes, all the men I never slept with."[139] Died in the Mull of Kintyre, Scotland, on January 11, 1999.

Montefiore, Sir Moses Haim. 101. British Jewish philanthropist. Died in London, England, on July 28, 1885.**

Montgomery, Joseph Tilden. 107. Described his recollections of early Montana history and the Spanish-American War in the book *Colonel Joe: The Last of the Rough Riders*. Died in Lewistown, Montana, on February 26, 1984.**

Moreno, Wenceslao. 103. Known as "Senor Wences." Ventriloquist who appeared 43 times on the *Ed Sullivan Show*. Famous for his gutteral "s'all right" and squeaky "s'OK" answers from Jimmy, his hand puppet. Born in Salamanca, Spain, where he learned to imitate voices as a schoolboy and to answer "present" for absent classmates. His teacher was not amused by his antics and made him stay after school to clean ink wells, providing him with the opportunity to make faces on his closed fist—the beginning of his act. His bizarre, farcical, Spanish-accented patter proved to be an immediate hit with television audiences. At age 90, he appeared in *Sugar Babies* with Mickey Rooney. On his 100th birthday, the Friars Club made him a lifetime member, and he received a Lifetime Achievement Award from the National Comedy Hall of Fame. Died in New York, New York, on April 21, 1999.

Morgan, Walter L. 100. Financial pioneer who founded the Wellington Mutual Fund, which today has 900,000 stockholders. Worked three days per week at his office until he broke a hip at age 99. Restored and supported the historic Morgan House, built by one of his ancestors in 1695. Honorary director of Philadelphia Orchestra and the Philadelphia Academy of Music. Last survivor of the Princeton class of 1920. Died in Bryn Mawr, Pennsylvania, on September 2, 1998.

Morse, True Delbert. 102. President of the Commodity Credit Corporation, the multibillion-dollar agricultural price support system, and Under Secretary of Agriculture for the Eisenhower administration. President of Doane Agricultural Service, a provider of farm appraisals, research reports and editorial information for publications. Served as head of the National Farm Committee for Thomas Dewey during his unsuccessful runs for the presidency in 1948 and 1952. Died in Sun City, Arizona, on June 3, 1998.

Mortensen, Christian. 115. Born in 1882 in Skarrup, Denmark, he came to the United States when he was 21. Claimed "a good cigar, lots of water, no alcohol and staying positive will keep you alive a long time."[140] Died in San Rafael, California, on May 2, 1998.

Moses, "Grandma" Anna Mary Robertson. 101. Painter. Died in Hoosick Falls, New York, on December 13, 1961.**

Nearing, Dr. Scott. 100. Professor at the Wharton School of the University of Pennsylvania. Socialist and author of numerous books including *The Twilight of Empire: An Economic Interpretation of Imperialist Cycles, Wages in the United States, Reducing the Cost of Living* and *The Super Race: An American Problem.* Died in Harborside, Maine, on August 23, 1983.**

Nyswander, Dr. Dorothy Bird. 104. Founder of the School of Public Health at the University of California at Berkeley. Served with the Federal Works Agency, playing a major role in setting up nursery schools and child care centers in 15 northeastern states. Her analysis of New York youngsters entitled "Solving School Health Problems" still is studied today in public health education courses. Conducted seminars at her home until she was 103. Mother of Marie Nyswander Dole, the psychiatrist who pioneered methadone treatments for heroine addicts. Died in Berkeley, California, on December 18, 1998.

Oku, Mumeo. 101. Pioneer in women's rights. Founder of the Housewives Association, one of Japan's first and most important consumer groups with 391 chapters. One of the first women to serve in Parliament, after years of campaigning for universal suffrage. Ran a home for impoverished women and children from 1923 to 1944. "She always wore a beautiful kimono, but her mind was tougher than that of a man," wrote an official from the Housewives Association.[141] Died in Tokyo, Japan, on July 9, 1997.

Provaznik, Marie. 100. Director of 1948 Czechoslovakian gymnastic team. President of the women's division of the International Gymnastics Federation of Geneva. Defected to the United States after the Communist takeover in 1948. Died in Schenectady, New York, on January 11, 1991.

Red Fox, Chief William. 105. Sioux whose memories of the Battle of the Little Bighorn and Wounded Knee stirred controversy. Died in Corpus Christi, Texas, on March 1, 1976.**

Roach, Harold Eugene. 100. Writer, producer and director who began his career as a $5-a-day cowboy extra. Pioneer of film comedy. Helped Will Rogers, Charley Chase, Harry Langdon and Harold Lloyd rise to stardom. Introduced the Laurel and Hardy and "Our Gang" comedies. Received three Academy Awards, including one in 1984 for lifetime achievement. An energetic man and a flashy dresser who once owned six planes and 20 polo ponies, Mr. Roach became a founder and president of the Los Angeles Turf Club. Died in Bel Air, California, on November 2, 1992.

Rudge, Olga. 101. Concert violinist who forsook her career to share her life with poet Ezra Pound, whom she met in 1916. The two lived together until 1945, when United States forces arrested Pound for anti-American propaganda during World War II. Miss Rudge campaigned for his release and arranged for the publication of his works while he was incarcerated. After Pound's release in 1958, the couple returned to Italy until the poet's death in 1972. She carefully guarded the poet's privacy from prying intruders, asking them to recite a line or two of his poetry before granting an audience. She complained that, although they embraced the wisdom of Ezra Pound, they hadn't read his work. Died in Merano, Italy, on March 15, 1996.

Schlink, Frederick J. 103. Cofounder of the Consumer's Club, which publicized unsafe and defective products tested at its Bowerstown, New Jersey, laboratory. Co-author of *Eat, Drink and Be Wary, Your Money's Worth* and the best-selling *100,000,000 Guinea Pigs,* an appeal for federal food and drug regulations. Died in Phillipsburg, New Jersey, on January 20, 1995.

Seldes, George. 104. Author of *Lords of the Press; The Truth behind the News; Iron, Blood and Profits; Eat;* and *Freedom of the Press.* Died in Windsor, Vermont, on July 2, 1995.**

Shinwell, Lord Emanuel. 101. British defense minister under Atlee's Labor government in 1950–1951. Dropped out of school at age 11 to work. His activities on behalf of trade unionism landed him in jail in 1919 for inciting dock workers to riot. Sought to protect the rights of the poor and downtrodden throughout his career. Spent 40 years in the House of Commons. Secretary for mines during World War II. In 1945, he became the minister for fuel and power. Named a baron in 1970 and served in the House of Lords thereafter. Author of *The Britain I Want*. Once aspired to become a prize fighter. When a conservative said, "Go back to Poland," a disparaging remark about his Jewish-Polish ancestry, Shinwell instantly crossed the floor and threw a punch at the offender. He was an inveterate pipe smoker who frequently enjoyed a glass of whiskey. Died in London, England, on May 8, 1986.

Shulman, Rebecca Beldner. 100. National president of Hadassah, a woman's Zionist organization. In 1947, she helped David Ben-Gurion, the chairman of the Jewish Agency for Palestine, break ground for a new Hadassah hospital on Mount Scopus. A trained nurse, Mrs. Shulman took a special interest in Hadassah's medical programs. Her eldest son, Paul, helped establish the Israeli Navy. Died in New York, New York, on March 30, 1997.

Smith, Major General Ralph. 104. Received flying lessons from Orville Wright. Became the 13th person in the United States to receive a pilot's license. Served with General John Pershing against Pancho Villa's Mexican revolutionaries as a young lieutenant. He earned a Silver Star for bravery in World War I. Taking command of the 27th Infantry in 1942, Smith's troops captured Makin Atoll in the Gilbert Islands. He became a military attaché to the American embassy in Paris after the war. Following retirement from the service in 1948, he became a fellow at Stanford University's Hoover Institute on War, Revolution and Peace. When asked by the press how he achieved such a great age, he explained, "I get up in the morning, and I'm still here."[142] Died in Palo Alto, California, on January 21, 1998.

Snyder, J. Roy. 101. Founder of New Castle Duntile, one of the earliest companies with ready-mix concrete trucks. Served on numerous charitable, religious and commercial boards and was famous for his homemade candied walnuts, which he sent out during the Christmas season. Died in Fort Lauderdale, Florida, on January 22, 1997.

Sopwith, Sir Thomas Octave Murdoch. 101. British aircraft pioneer. At age 22, he became the 31st British aviator to hold a flying certificate. Raised the money to bankroll his company by stunt flying, winning 4,000 pounds, about $20,000, for a flight across the British Channel. "We had lots of crashes in those days, but, bless you, it was fun."[143] His company produced more than 6,000 British Sopwith Camel planes during World War I, one of which shot down German ace Baron von Richthofen, nicknamed the "Red Baron." During World War II, Sopwith's Hawker Hurricanes downed hundreds of German bombers. Sir Thomas was knighted in 1953 for his contributions to aviation and the war effort. Died in Winchester, England, on January 27, 1989.

Stanley, Harry. 100. Vaudevillian turned lecturer. Doubletalk artist who frequently began his speeches with "For those of you who might have missed my introduction, I'm Professor Stanley, Harvard '39, Rutgers nothing." He dressed in a conservative suit and a pince-nez and looked the part of an expert while mouthing "erudite nonsense." Stanley appeared in numerous broadway shows including centenarian George Abbott's production of *Broken Wing*. Died at the Actor's Home in Englewood, New Jersey, on February 15, 1998.

Stickney, Dorothy. 101. Actress famous for her role as Vinnie Day in *Life with Father*, which ran for 3,183 performances on Broadway and was written by her husband and costar, actor, director and producer Howard Lindsay. Continued the character of Vinnie in the sequel, *Life with Mother*. Originally turned down for so many roles she wrote the poem *You're Not the Type*, which was published in *Liberty Magazine*. She played Liz, the mad scrubwoman in Chicago, the first play directed by centenarian George Abbott. She wrote *A Lovely Light*, a one-woman play based on the life of Edna St. Vincent Millay. In her memoir,

Openings and Closings, she confessed to suffering from severe stage fright all her life. Her father, a doctor who made house calls on horseback, became one of the first inductees into the Cowboy Hall of Fame. Died in Manhattan, New York, on June 2, 1998.

Stukelj, Leon. Born in November 1898. Winner of three Olympic gold medals in gymnastics in 1924 and 1928. Developer of the "Stukelj Cross" move on the parallel bars. After retiring from sports, he served as a judge in his homeland of Maribor, Slovenia. With two sisters who lived beyond 90 as well as a no-alcohol and no-tobacco lifestyle, Stukelj continued to exercise at the age of 100.

Taylor, Charles F. 101. Director of the Sloan Laboratory for Aircraft and Automotive Engines at the Massachusetts Institute of Technology. Aide to the Wright brothers during their early flights. Assisted in the design of the Spirit of St. Louis, the airplane that carried Charles Lindbergh across the Atlantic in 1927. Taylor's two-volume text *The Internal Combustion Engine in Theory and Practice* still remains the primary reference for automotive engineers. Created the Educational Counseling Committee, which helped send 2,000 underprivledged youths to college. When asked what it means to be 100, he responded, "I saw Haley's Comet twice, once in 1910 and once in 1986."[144] Died in Weston, Massachusetts, on June 22, 1996.

Turner, Dr. Thomas Wyatt. 101. Civil rights pioneer and professor emeritus of biology at Hampton Institute. Specialist in plant physiology and pathology. Founded the Federation of Colored Catholics to combat discrimination. Charter member of the National Association for the Advancement of Colored People and chairman of its first membership drive in Washington, D.C. "I didn't get up and start cussing people out, but I said things," he told reporters late in life.[145] He was a friend of key black leaders such as W. E. B. DuBois and Booker T. Washington. In 1976, the Secretariat of Black Catholics in Washington named its highest award in Dr. Turner's honor. Died in Washington, D.C., on April 21, 1978.

Van Fleet, General James A. 100. Opinionated but highly competent four-star army general. As a well-built six-footer, he played halfback for West Point's 1915 undefeated football team. Wounded as an infantry officer in the foxholes of World War I. Headed the assault landing at Omaha Beach during World War II. In 1945, he spearheaded the drive across Germany. Served as deputy chief of staff at the United States Army European command at Frankfurt. Became a central figure in the political storm of 1952 when he complained to Congress that he had been prohibited from waging a victory offensive in Korea and his troops lacked adequate ammunition. He retired in 1953, after almost 38 years of service. Recipient of the Distinguished Service Cross with three Oak Leaf Clusters. President Truman called him "the greatest general we have ever had. I sent him to Greece, and he won. I sent him to Korea, and he won."[146] His only son, Captain James Van Fleet Jr. was lost in action in Korea and presumed dead. The general served as a consultant to the Defense Department under President Kennedy and again attracted controversy by calling for the dismissal of Ambassador Adlai Stevenson for failing to support the invasion of Cuba at the Bay of Pigs. Died in Polk City, Florida, on September 23, 1992, and buried with full military honors at Arlington Cemetery.

Wedeck, Harry E. 102. Linguist, classical scholar and observer of the paranormal. Author of *A Dictionary of Aphrodiacs*, *A Treasury of Witchcraft*, *Dictionary of Astrology* and *A Triumph of Satan*. Chairman of classical languages at Erasmus High School in Brooklyn from 1935 to 1950, classics instructor at Brooklyn College until 1968 and lecturer on medieval studies at the New School of Research until 1974. Died in New York, New York, on July 8, 1996.

Weil, Joseph. 100. Confidence man known as the "Yellow Kid." Always immaculately groomed with a conservative suit, his trademark yellow gloves and a neatly trimmed Vandyke beard. He fixed prize fights, sold phony gold mines and kited nonexistent stock. His estimated take exceeded $8 million, and he spent time in jail on 40 occasions. Nattily attired in a flashy vest with a pearl stickpin, he explained on his 90th birthday, "I never fleeced anyone who could not afford to pay my price for a lesson in honesty. A truly honest man would never have fallen for my schemes."[147] He recorded his exploits in his *Autobiography of Yellow Kid Weil.* Died in Chicago, Illinois, on February 27, 1976.

Westheimer, Irvin Ferdinand. 101. Founder of the Big Brothers Organization who was inspired by the sight of a ragged boy and his dog rummaging through a garbage can in search of food in 1903. Headed Westheimer Brokers until it merged with Hayden, Stone. Governor James Rhodes presented him with Ohio's highest award in 1977. Died in Cincinnati, Ohio, on December 30, 1980.

Wood, Beatrice. 105. Author of *I Shock Myself.* Potter and friend to dancer Isadora Duncan, artists Brancusi and Duchamp and writer Edna St. Vincent Millay. Died in Ojai, California, on March 12, 1998.**

Yu Yue Tsu, Bishop Andrew. 100. Anglican "Bishop of the Burma Road," who befriended Allied soldiers during World War II. Religious director of Peking Union Medical College in China. Worked to negotiate the return of church property from the Japanese following the war. Served as general secretary of the National Office of the House of Bishops in Nanking in 1946. Fled to the United States after the Communist takeover in 1949. Died in Wilmington, Delaware, on April 13, 1986.

Zukor, Adolph. 103. Founded Famous Players' Film Company in 1912. Chairman of Paramount Pictures, Incorporated. Died in Los Angeles, California, on June 10, 1976.**

** A fuller biography can be found in Part I of the book.

Epilogue

"The reward for living is the living itself," wrote centenarian and philosopher Charles Hartshorne. While by no means complete, this list of one hundred 100-year-olds who have made a difference reflects that philosophy of living.

Regrettably, the author may have omitted or been forced to choose between several desirable 100-year-old candidates, but that merely provides a strong incentive to produce a second book on centenarians. However, each of the individuals selected has influenced the world in one way or another, mostly for the better, but a few for the worse. Please accept my wish that all my readers may experience a healthy, happy, and prosperous centenarian life.

If you know of, or are a centenarian, who has made a difference, please contact the author at the following address: Dale Richard Perelman, P.O. Box 630, New Castle, Pennsylvania 16103.

Notes

1. *New York Times Biographical Service,* 1 February 1995.
2. Ibid., 158.
3. *New York Times Biographical Service,* 23 September 1989.
4. Ibid., 905.
5. Larry Tye, *The Father of Spin: Edward L. Bernays and the Birth of Public Relations* (New York: Crown Publishers, 1998), 14.
6. Edward L. Bernays, *Biography of an Idea: Memoirs of Public Relations Counsel Edward L. Bernays* (New York: Simon & Schuster, 1965), 184.
7. Ibid., 252.
8. Ibid., 193.
9. Ibid., 322.
10. Ibid., 779.
11. Tye, *The Father of Spin*, 220.
12. Lawrence T. Carter, *Eubie Blake: Keys of Memory* (Detroit: Balamp Publishing, 1979), 23.
13. Ibid., 30.
14. Ibid., 32.
15. Ibid.
16. Ibid., 36.
17. Ibid., 102.
18. Ibid., 108.
19. George Burns, *The Third Time Around* (New York: G. P. Putnam's Sons, 1980), 67.
20. George Burns, *Gracie: A Love Story* (New York: G. P. Putnam's Sons, 1988), 13.
21. George Burns, *All My Best Friends* (New York: G. P. Putnam's Sons, 1989), 15.
22. Mary Jean Madigan, *Stueben Glass: An American Tradition in Crystal* (New York: Harry N. Abrams, Inc., 1982).
23. Cora Tope Clark, *Reminiscences of a Centenarian* (San Antonio: The Naylor Company, 1972), 17.

24. Ibid., 21–22.

25. Ibid., 82.

26. Sarah and Elizabeth Delany with Amy Hill Hearth, *Having Our Say: The Delany Sisters' First 100 Years* (New York: Kodansha International, 1993), 17.

27. Ibid., 73.

28. Ibid., 121.

29. Ibid., 199.

30. Ibid., 9–10.

31. Marjory Stoneman Douglas, *Voice of the River* (Englewood, Fla.: Pineapple Press, 1987), 63.

32. Ibid., 61.

33. Ibid., 128.

34. Ibid., 167.

35. Ibid., 170.

36. Ibid., 225.

37. Ibid., 226.

38. Ibid., 254.

39. Ibid., 258.

40. *New York Times Biographical Service,* 15 May 1998, 721.

41. Ibid.

42. Eleanor Dulles, *Eleanor Lansing Dulles, Chances of a Lifetime: A Memoir* (Englewood Cliffs, N.J.: Prentice-Hall, 1980), 37.

43. Leonard Mosley, *Dulles: A Biography of Eleanor, Allen and John Foster Dulles and Their Family Network* (New York: The Dial Press, 1978), 90.

44. Ibid., 344.

45. Dulles, *Chances of a Lifetime,* 305.

46. Ibid., 314.

47. Ibid., 322.

48. Hamilton Fish, *Memoir of an American Patriot* (Washington: Regnery Gateway, 1991), 61.

49. Sterling Seagrave, *The Soong Dynasty* (New York: Harper & Row, 1985), 34.

50. Ibid., 128.
51. Ibid., 258.
52. Emily Hahn, *The Soong Sisters* (Garden City, N.Y.: Doubleday, Doran & Company, 1941), 270.
53. Ibid., 271.
54. Rose Fitzgerald Kennedy, *Times to Remember* (Garden City, N.Y.: Doubleday & Company, 1974), 178.
55. Ibid., 307.
56. Ibid., 344.
57. Ibid., 429.
58. Ibid., 476.
59. Ibid., 510.
60. *New York Times Biographical Service,* 23 January 1995, 113.
61. Kennedy, *Times to Remember,* 520.
62. Frederick Palmer, *This Man Landon* (New York: Dodd, Mead & Company, 1936), 32.
63. Ibid., 62.
64. Ibid., 161.
65. Ibid., 278.
66. *New York Times Biographical Service,* 1038.
67. Ibid.
68. Lee Meriwether, *Postscript to My Long Life 1862–1964* (St. Louis: Artcraft Press, 1964), 23.
69. Ibid., 16.
70. Ibid., 38.
71. Ibid.
72. Ibid.
73. Ibid., 18.
74. Ibid., 40.
75. Ibid., 43–44.
76. Ibid., 13.
77. Ibid., 125.
78. Ibid., 53.
79. Ibid., 54.

80. Ibid., 93.
81. Ibid., 113.
82. Ibid., 59.
83. Ibid., 108.
84. Ibid., 76.
85. Ibid., 15.
86. Ibid.
87. Sonia and V. D. Lipman, *The Century of Moses Montefiore* (London: Oxford University Press, 1985), 12.
88. Ibid., 16.
89. Paul Goodman, *Moses Montefiore* (Philadelphia: The Jewish Publication Society, 1925), 59.
90. Lipman, *The Century of Moses Montefiore*, 135.
91. Ibid., 131.
92. Ibid., 258.
93. Ibid.
94. Ibid., 245.
95. Ibid., 242.
96. Claudia Brownlee, *Colonel Joe: The Last of the Rough Riders* (Hicksville, N.Y.: Exposition Press, 1978), 19.
97. Ibid., 32.
98. Ibid., 65.
99. Ibid., 78.
100. Ibid., 188.
101. Ibid., 89.
102. Ken B. Lewistown, "Colonel Joe Cashes in His Chips," *News Argus*, 4 March 1984.
103. Ibid.
104. Ibid.
105. Anna Mary Robertson Moses, *Grandma Moses: My Life's History* (New York: Harper and Brothers, 1948), 54.
106. Ibid., 124.
107. Martha Laing, *Grandma Moses: The Grand Old Lady of American Art* (Charlotteville, N.Y.: SamHar Press, 1972), 19.

108. Ibid., 18.

109. Ibid., 27.

110. Scott Nearing, *The Making of a Radical: A Political Autobiography* (New York: Harper and Row, 1972), 20.

111. Ibid., 86.

112. Ibid., 91.

113. Helen Nearing, *Light on Aging and Dying: Wise Words* (New York: Tilbury House, 1995).

114. Chief William Red Fox, *The Memoirs of Chief Red Fox* (New York: McGraw-Hill, 1971), 110.

115. Ibid., 124–125.

116. Ibid., 128.

117. George Seldes, *Witness to a Century: Encounters with the Noted, the Notorious and the Three SOBs* (New York: Ballantine Books, 1987), 306.

118. Ibid., 466.

119. Beatrice Wood, *I Shock Myself* (San Francisco: Chronicle Books, 1988), 5.

120. Ibid., 11.

121. Ibid., 33.

122. Ibid., 38.

123. Ibid., 110.

124. Ibid., 133.

125. *Youngstown Vindicator*, Art Section, 14 June 1998.

126. Helen Dudar, "Beatrice Wood in Her Second Century," *Smithsonian* (March 1994): 86.

127. Ibid., 92–93.

128. Marcia Forsberg, "Pots of Gold," *Modern Maturity* (March–April 1988).

129. Ibid.

130. Burns, *All My Best Friends*, 304–305.

131. *New York Times Biographical Service*, 18 December 1996, 1873.

132. *New York Times Biographical Service*, 5 August 1997, 1214.

133. *New York Times Biographical Service*, 30 May 1998, 818.

134. Gregg Easterbrook, "A Hundred Years of Thinking about God," *U.S. News & World Report* (23 February 1998): 61.

135. *New York Times Biographical Service,* 29 December 1972, 2183.

136. *New York Times Biographical Service,* 24 September 1998, 1542.

137. Ibid.

138. *New York Times Biographical Service,* 18 February 1998, 242.

139. *New York Times Biographical Service,* 16 January 1999, 74.

140. *New York Times Biographical Service,* 3 May 1998, 645.

141. *New York Times Biographical Service,* 9 July 1997, 1058.

142. *New York Times Biographical Service,* 26 January 1998, 124.

143. *New York Times Biographical Service,* 28 January 1989, 105.

144. *New York Times Biographical Service,* 30 June 1996, 958.

145. *New York Times Biographical Service,* 25 April 1978, 525.

146. *New York Times Biographical Service,* 24 September 1992, 1230.

147. *New York Times Biographical Service,* 27 February 1999, 311.

Bibliography

Abbott, George. *Mister Abbott*. New York: Random House, 1963.

Bergreen, Laurence. *As Thousands Cheer: The Life of Irving Berlin*. New York: Viking Penguin, 1990.

Bernays, Edward L. *Biography of an Idea: Memoirs of Public Relations Counsel Edward L. Bernays*. New York: Simon & Schuster, 1965.

Bernays, Edward L. *The Later Years: Public Relations Insights 1956–1986*. Rhineback, N.Y.: H & M Publishers, 1986.

Brownlee, Claudia J. *Colonel Joe: The Last of the Rough Riders*. Hicksville, N.Y.: Exposition Press, 1978.

Burns, George. *All My Best Friends*. New York: G. P. Putnam's Sons, 1989.

———. *Gracie: A Love Story*. New York: G. P. Putnam's Sons, 1980.

———. *The Third Time Around*. New York: G. P. Putnam's Sons, 1988.

Carter, Lawrence T. *Eubie Blake: Keys of Memory*. Detroit: Balamp Publishing, 1979.

Clark, Cora Tope. *Reminiscences of a Centenarian*. San Antonio: The Naylor Company, 1972.

Delany, Sarah and Elizabeth with Amy Hill Hearth. *Having Our Say: The Delany Sisters' First 100 Years*. New York: Kodansha International, 1993.

Douglas, Marjory Stoneman. *Voice of the River*. Sarasota, Fla.: Pineapple Press, 1987.

Dudar, Helen. "Beatrice Wood in Her Second Century." *Smithsonian* (March 1994), 86–93.

Dulles, Eleanor Lansing. *Eleanor Lansing Dulles, Chances of a Lifetime: A Memoir.* Englewood Cliffs, N.J.: Prentice-Hall, Inc., 1980.

Easterbrook, Gregg. "A Hundred Years of Thinking about God." *U.S. News & World Report* (23 February 1998), 61–65.

Ewen, David. *The Story of Irving Berlin.* New York: Henry Holt and Company, Inc., 1950.

"The Final Bow—Madame Chiang Kai-shek Makes Public Appearance in Washington, D.C." *New Yorker* (August 14, 1995).

Fish, Hamilton. *Memoir of an American Patriot.* Washington, D.C.: Regnery Gateway, 1991.

Furia, Philip. *Irving Berlin: A Life in Song.* New York: Schirmer Books, 1998.

Goodman, Paul. *Moses Montefiore.* Philadelphia: The Jewish Publication Society of America, 1925.

Hahn, Emily. *The Soong Sisters.* Garden City, N.Y.: Doubleday, Doran & Company, Inc., 1941.

Heymen, Jim. *One Hundred Over 100.* Golden, Colo.: Fulcrum Publishing, 1990.

Kennedy, Rose Fitzgerald. *Times to Remember.* Garden City, N.Y.: Doubleday and Company, 1974.

Kessler, Ronald. "The Sins of the Father." *Reader's Digest.* (April 1996).

Laing, Martha. *Grandma Moses: The Grand Old Lady of American Art*. Charlotteville, N.Y.: SamHar Press, 1972.

Leaf, Alexander. "Every Day Is A Gift When You Are Over 100." *National Geographic* 143, no. 1 (January 1973).

Lipman, Sonia and V. D. *The Century of Moses Montefiore*. London: Oxford University Press, 1985.

Lyons, Len, and Don Perlo. *Jazz Portraits: The Lives and Music of the Jazz Masters*. New York: William Morrow and Company, 1989.

Madigan, Mary Jean. *Steuben Glass: An American Tradition in Crystal*. New York: Harry N. Abrams, Inc., 1982.

McCorkle, Susanna. "Ragtime to Riches: The Rise of Our Greatest Songwriter. *American Heritage* (November 1988).

Meriwether, Lee. *Postscript to My Long Life, 1862–1964*. St. Louis: Artcraft Press, 1964.

Moses, Anna Mary Robertson. *Grandma Moses: American Primitive*. Edited by Otto Kallir. New York: The Dryden Press, 1946.

Moses, Anna Mary Robertson. *Grandma Moses: My Life's History*. New York: Harper and Brothers, 1948.

Mosley, Leonard. *Dulles: A Biography of Eleanor, Allen and John Foster Dulles and Their Family Network*. New York: The Dial Press/James Wade, 1978.

Nearing, Scott. *The Making of a Radical: A Political Autobiography*. New York: Harper and Row, 1972.

New York Times Biographical Service. New York: Arno Press, 1970–1999.

Palmer, Frederick. *This Man Landon.* New York: Dodd, Mead & Company, 1936.

Perrott, Paul, Paul Gardner, and James Plant. *Steuben: Seventy Years of American Glassmaking.* New York: Praeger Publishers, 1974.

Plaut, James. *Steuben Glass.* New York: Dover Publications, 1972.

Red Fox, Chief William. *The Memoirs of Chief Red Fox.* New York: McGraw-Hill Book Company, 1971.

Rockwell, Robert. *Frederick Carder and His Steuben Glass: 1903–1933.* West Nyack, N.Y.: Dexter Press, 1968.

Seagrave, Sterling. *The Soong Dynasty.* New York: Harper & Row, Publishers, 1985.

Seldes, George. *Witness to a Century: Encounters with the Noted, the Notorious and the Three SOB's.* New York: Ballantine Books, 1987.

Tye, Larry. *The Father of Spin: Edward L. Bernays and the Birth of Public Relations.* New York: Crown Publishers, 1998.

Wood, Beatrice. *I Shock Myself.* San Francisco: Chronicle Books, 1988.

Zukor, Adolph. *The Public Is Never Wrong.* New York: G. P. Putnam's Sons, 1953.

"People are living longer nowadays, which is great. We finally found something that pleases both us and the insurance companies. And it appears that more and more people are achieving the centenarian stage of their lives. If you don't believe me, just ask Willard Scott."

Bob Hope

"What an inspirational book! My philosophy as a psychic/medium is that no one 'dies,' so even if many of these remarkable souls did pass to the other side after the age of 100 or more, I'm sure they're still equally as active—equally as busy sharing their love, happiness and wisdom with their fellow sweet spirits in paradise."

Kenny Kingston
Legendary celebrity psychic

"In the nature of things, adjusted human beings yearn to live long. They are acutely keen to know about the biographies of the centenarians to discover from their lifestyles the elixir of longevity.

Centenarians, written by Mr. Dale Richard Perelman, is a lighthouse that illuminates one hundred landmarks of such biographies.

For the seekers who long to live long, the book is entertainingly beneficial reading."

Fahmy Attalah, Ph.D.
Author and clinical
psychologist

"Who among us that have enjoyed a happy, fulfilling life, do not long, wish, pray for what these centenarians have accomplished . . . love, fulfillment, productive time and activity surrounded by a good world, family and friends. I am considerably past the middle and hope I can reach their exclusive '100 Club.'

Thanks, Seven Locks Press, for bringing these wonderful fascinating personalities to our attention. A good study."

Margaret Burk
Author and co-founder of
Round Table West

"I'm looking forward to my 100-year mark, then my greatest goal will be realized: to have Willard Scott wish me a happy birthday."

Harriett Wieder
Author of *Breaking Through:*
The Political Journey of the
Honorable Harriett M. Wieder